This journal belongs to

_____

tPt

Psalms

POETRY
ON
FIRE

devotional journal

FOOTNOTES

BroadStreet
PUBLISHING

BroadStreet Publishing Group, LLC
Racine, WI 53403
www.broadstreetpublishing.com

Psalms: POETRY ON FIRE
Footnotes Devotional Journal

By Brian Simmons with Mark Stibbe
Edited by Nathanael White

ISBN-13: 978-1-4245-4992-4

Cover and interior design by Garborg Design Works, Inc.
www.garborgdesign.com

Printed in China

AT EACH AND EVERY SUNRISE YOU WILL HEAR MY VOICE

AS I PREPARE MY SACRIFICE OF PRAYER TO YOU.

EVERY MORNING I LAY OUT THE PIECES OF MY LIFE ON THE ALTAR

AND WAIT FOR YOUR FIRE TO FALL UPON MY HEART.

Psalm 5:3

Introduction

*T*he Psalms have been a comfort and joy to millions since David, Asaph, Solomon, the sons of Korah, and a few others penned this poetry on fire. These psalms express our deepest and strongest emotions and have the power to turn sighing into singing and trouble into triumph.

Much of Christianity has become so intellectualized that our emotions and artistic creativity are often set aside as unimportant in the worship of God. The Psalms free us to become emotional, passionate, sincere worshippers. These 150 poetic masterpieces give us an expression of faith and worship. They become a mirror to the heart of God's people in our quest to experience God's presence.

Within the book of Psalms is pure praise, prayers, and the wisdom of God. Take time to read the chapters recommended from *Psalms: Poetry on Fire*

(sold separately). Then reflect on the inspirational content in the following footnotes and respond through praise, prayer, and recording what God speaks to your heart.

May the Holy Spirit set your heart on fire as you read, receive, and give unto the Lord the glory due his name, answering the cry of David in Psalm 150:6,

Let everyone everywhere join in

The crescendo of ecstatic praise to Yahweh!

Dr. Brian Simmons

Lead translator, *The Passion Translation*

Growing in Intimacy

PSALMS 1-2

In Psalm 1, the writer teaches us the importance of "meditating each and every moment in the revelation of light" (v. 2). This means delving deeply and unceasingly into the treasures of God's Word, the Bible, just as God's Son did in his life here on the earth. Those who meditate on the Father's instructions grow in intimacy and as a result grow in productivity. Deeply rooted by the brooks of bliss, they bear fruit in every season. This is great news! God's Word, read relationally rather than religiously, leads us from barrenness to blessing.

Psalm 2 says this: "He has decreed over me, 'You are my favored Son'" (v. 7). These beautiful words were first decreed over David and then declared by the Father over the Messiah Jesus in the River Jordan. In this powerfully anointed worship song of David, revelatory words about our sonship are uttered from heaven. Those who have received their adoption in Christ and by the Holy Spirit know God as Father can receive these words too. You and I can rest in the affirmation that we are the favored sons and daughters of God. This revelation comes to us from God's Word.

Ask your Father to move in your heart so that you read his letters to you for intimacy and not just for information. Then read these psalms again, letting the Holy Spirit reveal his heart behind the words he wrote. What is he showing you?

A Father Who Responds

PSALMS 3-4

*M*any people wrongly believe that God is remote from creation and apathetic to our cries. But that is not the way the Bible talks about God. In Psalm 3, we see David crying out to God for help when many are slandering him, seeking to imprison him in shame. But then David decrees: "I have cried out to you and from your holy presence, you send me a Father's help" (v. 4). When his sons and daughters are in trouble, Father God comes to their help. When they are shamed by wicked words, he honors them with kind words. Whatever your problems are right now, hold on to the Father's promises: help is on the way.

*I*n Psalm 3, David proclaimed that God was his shield. Here in Psalm 4, he declares that God is his "Champion Defender" (v. 1). There are times in the life of every child of God when trouble and persecution comes, when we feel "squeezed again" and we need a touch of God's kindness. We only need to wait. David tells us, "The Lord works wonders for every one of his chosen lovers" (v. 3). What a beautiful truth that is! If you're feeling squeezed right now, make this declaration: "It's only a matter of time before the light of the Father's radiant face will break through and my Champion Defender will show up!"

Write down those areas of your life in which you urgently need the help of your heavenly Father. Release your decree over each one that he is your Champion Defender.

Passionate Praying

PSALMS 5-6

Have you ever noticed how passionate David is in the Psalms? His words are not religious and ritualistic, devoid of emotion and sincerity. They are full of raw honesty. Look at Psalm 5: "Listen to my passionate prayer! Can't you hear my groaning?" (v. 1). David prays with fire in his bones. As a result, God answers in kind with fire. This is why David declares, "Every morning I lay out the pieces of my life on the altar and wait for your fire to fall upon my heart" (v. 3). David knows that his passion attracts the Father's presence. Will you open up your heart to the fire of God today?

In Psalm 6, David is oppressed on every side. His health is failing. He feels close to death's door, so he pleads with God not to let him die, saying, "Those who are in the graveyards sing no songs" (v. 5). What a statement that is! No wonder the Father answers David's prayer for help. God simply cannot resist the person whose heart is set to love him extravagantly. Maybe you're in a season of difficulty right now. Set your love on the Father. Pour out your heart and your desire for restoration to him. Believe that you too will be able to declare, "Yes! The Lord my Healer has heard all my pleading" (v. 9).

Consider the intimacy David shows with the Father. In what way does this inspire you to build the same intimacy with your Father?

_____

_____

_____

_____

_____

_____

_____

_____

_____

_____

_____

_____

_____

_____

_____

_____

_____

_____

Looking Up to Heaven

PSALMS 7-8

When we talk about passion for God, this can denote so many different things. In Psalm 7, we see David expressing a deeply emotional plea to God to vindicate him. He has been enduring great injustice at the hands of his oppressors. So he wraps himself in the Father's presence and calls out for justice. Instead of emoting publicly against his enemies, he emotes privately before God, and he makes sure to end in praise of the One who makes everything right in the end. Let's cry out for justice in the secret place. And when we are very low, let's agree to worship "the God of the Highest Place!" (v. 17).

From the low place of lamentation in Psalm 7, David now ascends to the high place of adoration in Psalm 8. In both psalms, David proves himself to be a passionate worshiper—passionate in pain in Psalm 7; passionate in praise in Psalm 8. As he adores God, he says, "Strength rises up" (v. 2). This is always what happens when we look up to the heavens when things are bleak on the earth. We see God's "creative genius glowing in the heavens" (v. 3). We catch a glimpse of the majesty of our Creator. We see how much honor he has bestowed on us as his children. Such worship is powerful. "This kind of praise has the power to shut Satan's mouth" (v. 2). Let's shut Satan's mouth today with some high praise.

Look at God's creation and write down everything you see that points to
the creative genius of God. Then turn that into passionate praise.

Responding to Injustice
PSALMS 9-10

*W*hen you're in the valley of oppression, it is so easy to react based on circumstances rather than responding according to the realities of heaven. One way to respond in the Spirit is to thank God. In Psalm 9, King David explodes with thanksgiving. Even though David is feeling oppressed, he thanks God for his marvelous miracles, for his wonderful vindication, and for his perfect protection. Above all, he thanks God that he doesn't forget those who are forgotten by others and that he will punish those who commit acts of injustice against the weak. That's a great response. Make this your declaration today: I will always express my heartfelt gratitude to God, even in times of trouble.

*T*here are times in all of our lives when we ask, "Why do those who deny God's authority and even his existence seem to prosper?" This is David's cry in Psalm 10. The wicked exalt themselves rather than God, parading their wealth rather than praising God. Such people seem to be so successful. Yet this is not the end of the story. They are completely unaware that "the Exalted God they deny will soon declare their doom!" (v. 5). When they oppress the poor, they forget that God is "famous for being the Helper of the fatherless" (v. 14). Let's agree to do what David did—let's turn our incomprehension into intercession and cry out to the Lofty One to hear the cries of the oppressed.

What situations in your life and in the world do you find
perplexing right now? Bring these situations to the
Father in a spirit of thanksgiving and intercession.

_____

_____

_____

_____

_____

_____

_____

_____

_____

_____

_____

_____

_____

_____

_____

_____

Reacting and Responding
PSALMS 11–12

There are times when we are tempted to "fly away like a bird to hide in the mountains for safety" (Psalm 11:1). Clearly David was in this situation in Psalm 11. He was in a time of persecution, and his friends were all saying, "Run away!" But David didn't look to his circumstances for direction; he looked to the Lord. He declares that God alone is his Hiding Place and that he trusts in the reigning King who cannot be shaken. He stands and fights in praise, declaring, "His heavenly rule will prevail" (v. 4). We sometimes face difficult circumstances. When these come, like David, we know that our Father will prevail, so we follow him no matter what surrounds us.

When we are oppressed, we can choose to react to our circumstances or respond to what we see our Father doing. In Psalm 12, we can see the warrior, fighting spirit emerge in David's prayers. Here he contends in prayer for justice to prevail. While the wicked use human words as weapons to destroy the oppressed, David rises up in warfare prayer and uses God's words as a sword to disarm the oppressor: "For every word God speaks is sure and every promise pure. . . . It's pure as sterling silver" (v. 6). So raise your silver sword today. No matter how bleak your circumstances appear to be, contend for them in prayer. Declare over them the words of God, "I will arise!" (v. 5).

God wants to hear what's really going on in your heart.
Speak to your Father from the heart today.

From Depression to Delight

PSALMS 13-14

Sometimes it's really difficult to pray with passion when your soul is downcast and you're feeling depressed. David was clearly in this situation in Psalm 13. What is so admirable is that he didn't give up on his conversations with God. He kept choosing to pray. More admirable still, he makes a choice to ask God for light rather than focusing on the darkness. He prays, "Bring light to my eyes in this pitch-black darkness" (v. 3). Most admirable of all, David positions himself in his spirit on the far side of God's answer to his prayer. He decrees, "I will sing my song of joy" (v. 6). If you are in a dark place right now, let God transport your heart and focus to his place of light.

One of the keys to transitioning from depression to delight is choosing to look up, not down. This is what David does in Psalm 14. As he looks up, he sees that "the Lord looks down in love, bending over heaven's balcony, looking over all of Adam's sons and daughters" (v. 2). This transforms everything. On earth, all David can see is the wicked prospering. But choosing to look up, he sees the Divine Lover looking down! He comes to see that "the Lord is on the side of the generation of loyal lovers" (v. 5). This in turn leads him to end his song with hope rather than despair. If you are tempted to look down, look up today instead. Seeing your Father's love will begin to turn your heart around.

If you feel like you're in a wilderness right now, compose a
new song (or lyrics to a song). Write down how you're feeling,
but choose to look up rather than down. Encourage your soul to soar!

Living in the Shining Place

PSALMS 15–16

Where you live can affect your soul. If you dwell in the slums, you can feel downcast. If you dwell in the mountains, you can feel uplifted. All this makes the invitation of Psalm 15 compelling. How about dwelling in the shining place where the Father dwells? Those who are wholehearted for God can live there. They never speak ill of others. They always speak out against injustice. They make their hearts a holy place and therefore have access to God's holy place. Jesus is supremely the one who fulfills this picture. But we can be like him and find our heart's true home in the radiant presence of God.

It is a truly comforting thing to know that there is a safe house you can go to in times of trouble. For David, God Almighty was his "Safe Place" (Psalm 16:1). He knew that God's holy lovers have the keys to this safe house. They can hide there any time, dwelling in the secure and protective presence of the Father. This is a pleasant place reserved for those whose desire is to fulfill God's desires. It is a place where God's whispers in the night bring wisdom and guidance, leading holy lovers to fulfill their destinies. It is a place where the Father is always close and available, where his wraparound presence is felt all of the time. Make it your aim to live here in your spirit every day!

What do you think the shining Safe Place is like—where your Father's wraparound presence is felt? Ask your Father today to show you that place, and envision yourself there in your spirit.

_____

_____

_____

_____

_____

_____

_____

_____

_____

_____

_____

_____

_____

_____

_____

_____

_____

God's Holy Lovers

PSALMS 17–18

*H*ave you ever been woken up in the night and felt the fire of God cleanse you through and through? From Psalm 17, we can see that David knew this experience. "In a visitation of the night you inspected my heart and refined my soul in fire" (v. 3). Loving our Father passionately draws us near to his fire of love that refines us, not by our trying extra hard to be righteous, but by his fire removing impurities from within. He melts down strongholds of deception and burns away addictions to sin, leaving us free to express our devotion to him. The whole focus is love, and love is the end result—purer love experienced by us and expressed by us.

*T*hose who set their hearts on purity and integrity have a great reward in store. According to Psalm 18 (a song that also appears in 2 Samuel 22), God steps down from heaven and takes hold of his godly lovers on the earth when they're in trouble. He rescues them and sets them in a broad place because he is so delighted by their fervor for staying pure. If you think about it, the Father did this for Jesus when he reached down from heaven after the crucifixion and raised him from the tomb. What a Father! Let's keep our hearts clean before God. Let's adore him as holy lovers, crying out with David, "Lord, I passionately love you. I want to embrace you" (v. 1).

Reflect on what any of these descriptions of God mean to you: my Power; Bedrock beneath my feet; Castle on a cliff; my forever firm Fortress; my Mountain of hiding; my Pathway of escape; my Tower of rescue; my secret Strength and Shield; Salvation's Ray of Brightness; always the Champion of my cause.

_____

_____

_____

_____

_____

_____

_____

_____

_____

_____

_____

_____

_____

_____

_____

Living a Life of Childlike Trust
PSALMS 19–20

To be a God lover you have to trust that God is real. Where then is such a trust grounded? According to Psalm 19, it is grounded in two things: first, the evidence of God's creation. "Space itself speaks his story every day" (v. 1). The whole world can hear the silent gospel message in creation's craftsmanship. Second, there is the written Word of God through which even the simplest soul can understand God's ways. To be a passionate God lover involves trust. But our trust is well grounded in the revelation of what God has made and what God has written. Declare over yourself today that you will trust the Father revealed in the stars, the Scriptures, and supremely in the Savior, Jesus Christ.

Psalm 20 is a song of trust. It is a celebration of the God who is worthy of our trust because he answers our prayers in miraculous ways. While many people on the earth put their trust in wisdom and weapons, "our boast is in the Lord our God who makes us strong and gives us victory" (v. 7). Worldly people may boast about their material and intellectual resources, but God-lovers brag about the faithfulness of God. The person whose heart is aligned to God's heart can say with David, "I know God gives me all that I ask for" (v. 6). What a wonderful promise to claim today.

Remind yourself of the many ways that God has been trustworthy in your life. Write your own psalm of trust.

Celebrating the Messiah

PSALMS 21-22

Psalm 21 was originally a song of joy in which David celebrated the blessings that God bestowed on Israel's king. But like the Psalms as a whole, this worship song also points ahead to Jesus and celebrates the blessings God the Father bestowed on his Son. So celebrate today the way God gave Jesus the desire of his heart—you and me! Celebrate the way God has made Jesus famous throughout the earth—far more famous than any other person in history. Celebrate the fact that Jesus is the King of Kings and that God has given him a royal crown of gold and garments of glory. Make it your aim to go on praising King Jesus, who is strong, mighty, and all-powerful.

The path to Jesus' exaltation as King of Kings was a path of excruciating pain. Jesus went to hell and back for you and me. David prophesies about this in Psalm 22. He takes us deep into the passion of Christ, including his desperate cries and unstoppable sobbing. He gives us a glimpse of the agony of Jesus when he feels in his breaking human heart that his Father in heaven has abandoned him. He shows us Christ crushed, bleeding crimson—abused, despised, and scorned by all. There are many prophecies of the passion found in this Psalm, including in its final words, "It is finished!" (v. 31). As you look at the passion of Jesus, let his passion for you stir the fires of your passion for him.

Reflect on the many sufferings prophesied about Christ Jesus by David in Psalm 22. Ask the Holy Spirit to help you understand Christ's love behind his actions, and express your gratitude and love for his sacrifice.

The Shepherd King

PSALMS 23-24

*W*hen he composed Psalm 23, David reached the highest heights of lyrical beauty and spiritual adoration. Having been a shepherd himself, David gives eloquent praise to the Shepherd Lord. The Shepherd Lord extolled by David offers him a resting place in his luxurious love and leads him to oases of peace, brooks of bliss. All this is true for us too. As followers of the Messiah Jesus (the Good Shepherd to whom David is pointing), we too can say, "I'll never be lonely, for you are near" (v. 4). We too can say that we are pursued by love. Worship the Good Shepherd today.

*T*he Messiah to whom David points in Psalm 23 is not only Shepherd, but he is also King. David himself had known both roles. He had been a shepherd as a boy and a king as a man. Here in Psalm 24, he enlists all his spiritual passion and poetic art to magnify the Glory King, the Mighty One, the invincible Commander of heaven's hosts. He encourages us to have pure and undivided hearts so that we can welcome the coming of the King of Glory. Above all, he exhorts us to hunger after the presence of this Glory King. Choose today that you will always be one of those who seeks the pleasure of King Jesus' face.

"You anoint me with the fragrance of your Holy Spirit" (Psalm 23:5).
Write a prayer asking to be covered in the perfume of the Glory King.

_____

_____

_____

_____

_____

_____

_____

_____

_____

_____

_____

_____

_____

_____

_____

_____

_____

When You Feel Condemned

PSALMS 25-26

In Psalm 25, David is struggling with shame. He thinks back over his life and remembers the sins of his past. He asks that the Father will give him grace and look at him through eyes of love. "Never count my sins and forgive them all," he cries (v. 11). David, of course, lived before Jesus' blood was shed at Calvary. Aren't you thankful for the certainty that when you repent, there is no charge against you in heaven? We live on the right side of the cross and can be sure of God's mercy. We can rest with our loving Father and hear his revelation secrets. When you bring your shame to the Lord, know that he will lift your burdens from you and restore intimacy.

Have you ever felt unjustly accused by someone? David clearly knew this experience. In Psalm 26, he laments the fact that his name has been bad-mouthed and his reputation sullied by scheming sinners. Yet David says he has done his best to keep God's laws and he has chosen to make his home in God's presence rather than sinners' hangouts. So he makes a choice to trust in God to clear his name. He decides not to use his human resources to try to orchestrate justice. He trusts without wavering in God and relies solely on the vindication that God alone can bring. If you're facing unjust accusation, put your trust in God's vindication and turn worrying into worship.

What injustice have you experienced or may be experiencing today?
Write out your thankfulness to your Father that he is near
to you in good times and bad.

_____

_____

_____

_____

_____

_____

_____

_____

_____

_____

_____

_____

_____

_____

_____

_____

_____

Orphans No More

PSALMS 27-28

In Psalm 27:10, David says, "My father and mother abandoned me. I'm like an orphan." Then he goes on to say to God, "But you took me in and made me yours." God became a Father to David, giving him the four things every child needs from a parent: acceptance, attention, direction, and protection. All these things David describes in verses 7–14. Above all, he declares that he has found "the privilege of living with him every moment in his house" (v. 4). He has found *home*. Thanks to Jesus, the same is true for us. We are no longer orphans. We have found our heart's true home in him. Praise God you're not an orphan anymore (John 14:18).

Orphans live from a center of fear. Sons and daughters live from a center of love. In Psalm 27, David declared, "My heart will not be afraid" (v. 3). Now in Psalm 28, David hides himself in the wraparound presence of God during a time of exile. He declares that God is his Strength and Shield from every danger. Notice here the choices that David makes during a time of isolation and deprivation. He doesn't react like an orphan and wallow in fear. He responds like a son and rests in the assurance that the Father loves him. Ask God to fill you afresh with his Spirit of Adoption so you can have confidence even beyond David's.

If you have not yet truly found your home in God's presence,
ask the Holy Spirit to fill you afresh, take you deeper into himself,
and reveal to you the truth that you are his child.

Balanced Worshipers

PSALMS 29–30

*H*ow balanced is your picture of God? One of the most impressive things about David's songs of worship is that they portray God as awesome in unparalleled power on the one hand and tender in intimate love on the other. Psalm 29 is a great example. Here God is exalted as the one whose voice thunders from heaven. Seven times David extols "the voice of the Lord" for its mountain-shaking power (seven is the number that symbolizes perfection in Jewish thought). At the same time, God is praised for giving us the kiss of peace. David's God is both far and near, fearful and kind, royal and relational. What a wonderful God we have who has made us his children!

*B*alanced worshipers know that the Father not only embraces his people, he sometimes chastises them too. In Psalm 30, David shows once again that he's a balanced worshiper. He knows that God can sometimes be angry because of our sins. But he also knows that God's loving favor lasts a lifetime. We may therefore have to weep through the night at times. But at daybreak we experience ecstatic joy. At times it may feel as though God hides his presence from us, but as we turn our hearts to him again, he restores us to the glory of gladness.

Which attributes of God do you focus on most often? Give time now to those you have normally given less attention to. Worship and praise him, and as you do, let him reveal even more of his wonder to you.

_____

_____

_____

_____

_____

_____

_____

_____

_____

_____

_____

_____

_____

_____

_____

_____

_____

_____

My Hiding Place on High
PSALMS 31–32

Have you ever been in a season of your life where the only option was to hide yourself in God? David was in this predicament when he penned Psalm 31. He was being overwhelmed by his enemies and insulted by brutal people. What was his response? As one of God's beloved ones, he knew there was a secret and a safe place where he could hide. So he tucked himself away in the tabernacle of God's presence and there turned all his laments into love songs. He resolved to love the Lord with passion and to wait for him to break through. If that's something you need to do, resolve to cheer up and take courage in God your strong Shelter and your Hiding Place on high.

According to Psalm 32, the key to God's hiding place is integrity. David had broken the commandments when he committed adultery with Bathsheba and then murdered her husband. After refusing to repent, he eventually surrendered to God. God's hand of conviction had been heavy on David's heart, causing him no end of inner turmoil, but when David relented and repented, God completely forgave him and wiped the slate clean. David now knew for sure that he would be kept safe when the storms of life threatened. Only those who exhibit integrity and transparency before God can declare, "You are my secret Hiding Place" (v. 7). Make a new commitment to being real before God today.

Are you carrying any burdens in your soul right now—burdens caused by unconfessed sin? Write a prayer of confession and enjoy the feeling of your burdens being removed and God becoming your Hiding Place once again.

_____

_____

_____

_____

_____

_____

_____

_____

_____

_____

_____

_____

_____

_____

Sing a New Song
PSALMS 33–34

It is so easy to forget that the book of Psalms is a stunning collection of worship songs. This was King David's greatest joy. Before he was a leader, he was a lover. Before he was a warrior, he was a worshiper. This is so evident in Psalm 33 where David exhorts us to "compose new melodies" (v. 3). He urges us to allow the Creator God to inspire us with creativity and to come up with a new song—a spontaneous composition of uninhibited adoration. He encourages us to take the anointing and skill God has given us and use that to sing and shout with passion. So take hold of the Word of God, maybe one of his promises, and with all you've got inside, turn your passion into poetry.

You might say, "It is easy to be passionate in praise when life is good. What about when times are hard?" David gives us the answer in Psalm 34, a song he composed at the worst moment in his life. David was on the run, devoid of friends, and hiding in a cave. But even here a tune begins to form in his trouble. He remembers all God's done for him in the past, and all of a sudden his misery turns to music and he's bursting with joy! Angels encircle and empower him as he praises God. He is not alone! Heaven comes down as his praises go up. His passionate pursuit attracts the presence of God, showing us that our trials can become a testimony and our testimony a thanksgiving.

Whatever creative skill God has given you, use it now. Pen a poem, sing a song, paint a picture, drum on a table, or do whatever you can do. Use your God-given creativity to look away from your trouble and pursue God passionately and artistically.

_____

_____

_____

_____

_____

_____

_____

_____

_____

_____

_____

_____

_____

_____

_____

_____

Journeying in Prayer
PSALMS 35-36

It has been said that prayer doesn't change God but it does change you. Nowhere is this more evident than in Psalm 35 where David is facing dire difficulties once again, enduring slander and attacks from those for whom he had so fervently interceded. He begins as a warrior, asking God to arise in his armor and to bring him deliverance. Then he becomes a witness, giving testimony to how the very people he had once blessed were now seizing on his stumbling to tear him to shreds. Finally, he becomes a worshiper, declaring that "the Lord will be glorified in it all!" (v. 27). What a journey within just one song of praise! Let's not try to change God. Let's allow God to change us in prayer.

When we bring our honest feelings to God, his presence enables us to transition from lamentation to celebration. Psalm 36 is a vivid example of this. In verses 1-4, David deplores the spiritual blindness he can see all around him. He laments the sinful rebellion in the world. Then in verse 5, instead of focusing on human failings, David turns his attention to the limitless love of God. Not even a mouse is beyond the reach of this tender love. Instead of focusing on man's sin, David transitions to a contemplation of God's grace. There's a lesson here for all of us: when we are very real with God in prayer, we need to allow God to change our perspective from the sins of others to the splendors of God.

Be real with God about the worst thing happening in your life right now, yet as you speak to him about this, let him shift your focus from your problem to the promise that he is with you.

_____

_____

_____

_____

_____

_____

_____

_____

_____

_____

_____

_____

_____

_____

_____

_____

_____

The Stature of Waiting

PSALMS 37–38

*T*here have probably been times in all of our lives when we've looked at the wealth of the ungodly and thought they were better off than us. David puts this idea to rest in Psalm 37. He tells us not to envy the wealthy but to fix our eyes on God's promises. He is a faithful Provider. If we trust him, he will bless us. The key is to realize that it is better to have little materially but a lot with God. Our task is to grab hold of the promise that we will always have more than enough even in a recession and wait for God to provide. God-lovers never see their children go hungry. So wait patiently to be blessed, then be generous with your abundance!

*H*ave you ever noticed how often David teaches us to "wait upon the Lord" in the Psalms? The Hebrew word translated *wait* means literally "to tie together by entwining or wrapping tightly." In Psalm 38, David says that he is spiritually broken because of his sins and physically wrecked because of sicknesses. In the midst of this torment, David declares, "Lord, the only thing I can do is wait and put my hope in you. I wait for your help, my God" (v. 15). Maybe you need God's help right now. Waiting for the Lord is not passive. It is a process of tying yourself to the Father's promises in prayer. How can you tie yourself to your Father today?

Consider the image of tying yourself to the Father, entwining your heart with his promises. This is what waiting involves. Turn this beautiful word picture into a prayer for help from God.

_____

_____

_____

_____

_____

_____

_____

_____

_____

_____

_____

_____

_____

_____

_____

_____

_____

_____

From Weeping to Rejoicing
PSALMS 39–40

*H*ave you ever been so deeply moved by your frailty and failures that you've wept before the Lord? If you have, you're in good company. If Psalm 39 is anything to go by, David went through times like these. In this psalm it is the sense of his mortality that has overwhelmed him. The life of a human being is a puff of air, a fleeting shadow. All our energy is invested in things that are here today, gone tomorrow. Recognizing his own weakness, David offers up his tears as liquid prayers. He ends by asking that God would not let him die before experiencing joy once again. Moments like these help us keep perspective on what's really important—those things that last forever. Don't wait for difficulties to remember that our time on earth is short. Consider it now, and focus your heart on heavenly things.

*D*avid ended Psalm 39 with a prayer that God would move from frowning on his failures to smiling over his success. From the start of Psalm 40, we can see how God answers this kind of heartfelt prayer. David isn't weeping anymore. He is laughing. Tears in the night have turned to joy in the morning. After a period of waiting on the Lord, David experiences his breakthrough and a new song of ecstatic praise, for a new day rises up in his heart. "Blessing after blessing comes to those who love and trust the Lord" (v. 4). So from weeping David turns to rejoicing, revealing that he is a man of spiritual passion. Let's ask the Holy Spirit to give us the heart of David.

Nearly every great revival in history has begun with someone somewhere weeping before the Lord. Their personal revival so often led to a corporate revival in their community.
Ask the Holy Spirit to give you the gift of tears.

Holy Desperation

PSALMS 41–42

There has never been a great move of God that hasn't been preceded by a group of people who became desperate for more of God's presence. Psalm 41 begins with the revelation that God has a special place in his heart for those who are poor and helpless, who only have God and nothing else. When David was sick, he said he cried out to God, "I need you." That's the cry of a man who is desperate. God is not holding out on anyone, but he simply waits for people who invite him to come, people who genuinely want his presence. And when he comes, he always brings healing and restoration. Let's pray for the Kind Healer to come and revive us again.

Revival begins with a passionate cry for the presence of the Lord. David shows us how at the start of Psalm 42. He cries, "My soul thirsts, pants, and longs for the Living God" (v. 2). He says that day and night his tears keep falling because he is so thirsty for God's presence. He remembers days when he led the people of God in procession and the sound of passionate celebration filled the air. He pines for those times. The deep places of his heart cry out to the deep kindness in God's. He hangs tenaciously on to the promises of God and stirs himself to sing the praises of God. What an example David is to all who long for revival.

Write a prayer or compose a song-poem to express your holy
desperation for more of your Father's presence.

Encouraging Yourself in the Lord
PSALMS 43-44

$\mathcal{D}$id David have access to uplifting podcasts? No, nor were any other modern resources available to him—Christian TV, DVDs, books, Bible study apps, and so forth. As Psalm 43 vividly shows, David had only one way of turning his downcast soul into a rejoicing soul. He had to encourage and strengthen himself in the Lord. When David felt oppressed and depressed, he spoke to his own soul, telling himself not to be disturbed but to expect God to break through. Perhaps we have a lot to learn about the art of encouraging ourselves in the Lord from David. Let's cultivate a lifestyle of speaking to the soul within, calling it into strength and encouragement in the Lord.

$\mathcal{O}$ne of the ways we can encourage ourselves in the Lord is by remembering the great things God has done for us in the past. This is what David does in Psalm 44. He reminds himself how God gave his ancestors the Promised Land by the shining of God's radiant presence. Although things now look bleak, David remembers that it was not by human strength but by God's power that they received the promise. When times are difficult (as they were for David here), we can strengthen ourselves in the Lord by declaring, "God, we've heard about all the glorious miracles you've done" (v. 1). Then our soul springs to life and we can decree, "You are my God, my King!" (v. 4).

Practice speaking to your own soul right now.

Command it to be encouraged in the Lord.

Remind yourself of the greatest displays of God's power you've seen.

The Bridegroom and Warrior

PSALMS 45–46

Psalm 45 is a nuptial song. David portrays a wedding day celebration between the Bridegroom Messiah (the Son of David to come, Jesus Christ) and the bride (the church). Using "beautiful lyrics," David first makes poetic and prophetic declarations about the Bridegroom, "the most wonderful and winsome of men" (vv. 1–2). Then he turns to the princess bride, exhorting her to lay aside every previous attachment and devote herself to her Royal Bridegroom. This Bridegroom King has showed his great passion at Calvary and carries "the scent of suffering love" (v. 8). As the bride, let yourself be carried away by the aroma of sacrificial love in the presence of the Lord.

The Messiah whom David is prophetically extolling in Psalms 45 and 46 is not only the Royal Bridegroom. He is also, in Psalm 46, the Commander of the armies of heaven. Our husband Jesus Christ is the Warrior King of Kings! We therefore don't have to live in fear when the nations rage against each other. Even though the world may sometimes be in turmoil, Jesus is on the throne in heaven, in the City of God Most High, where sparkling streams bring his people joy. Whenever we are tempted to be dismayed by the traumas and tragedies of this world, we should gaze upon our Bridegroom Warrior. Rest in the revelation of his unsurpassable power and exchange worry for wonder.

Write down every title of the Bridegroom and Warrior Messiah
in these two Psalms and turn it into passionate praise of Jesus,
with your "heart on fire" (Psalm 45:1).

Adoring Our King

PSALMS 47-48

*H*ow passionate is your praise? How effusive is your worship? In both your private encounters with God and in public worship in the church, we should express our adoration with our hearts, hands, feet, and voices. This is certainly what Psalm 47 encourages. We are urged to clap our hands and utter raucous shouts of joy! The Messiah is the most formidable of kings. He is the triumphant King who rules over the nations. How can we remain passive and indifferent in the light of such a royal revelation? God never said that he *inhibited* the praises of his people. He said that he *inhabited* them. Maybe, like David, we can become a whole lot more passionate—more undignified than we have been in the past.

*A*re you ever lost for words when you worship the King of Kings? You should be! There simply aren't enough finite words to begin to describe our infinite King! So the writer of Psalm 48 begins by confessing that "there are so many reasons to describe God as wonderful" (v. 1). The King of Kings reigns in his heavenly city (of which Zion in Israel's history was an earthly counterpart). Just as the Assyrian army came against Jerusalem and was defeated in the time this psalm was written, so every enemy that seeks to attack God will be blown away. So rest secure before the throne of the King in the City of our God. He cannot be either defeated or moved. We should always be lost for words as we celebrate "our incomparable King" (v. 2).

What does "undignified" look like to you? Do something to worship your Father with unrestrained passion today! You may feel foolish, but let loose!

_____

_____

_____

_____

_____

_____

_____

_____

_____

_____

_____

_____

_____

_____

_____

_____

The Wisdom and Word of God

PSALMS 49–50

*H*ave you ever had the experience of uttering wisdom that you knew was from heaven? David clearly did. He constantly moved in a realm of the Spirit in which he turned mysteries into music and riddles into rhymes. His experience, according to Psalm 49, was that he often received wisdom from God, words of understanding and insight. These he turned into the praise poems we know as the Psalms. For David, this wisdom was far more valuable than all the wealth in the world. This wisdom from heaven contains within it the priceless secret of a soul's redemption. Death robs a rich man of his wealth but cannot rob a poor man of this wisdom. Always seek to pursue wisdom more than wealth.

*A*ll other deities on the planet are dumb because they are lifeless, but the God of David speaks because he is alive forever. That's the chant of David in Psalm 50. The Living God speaks all the time. He speaks through every beautiful sunset and every earsplitting rumble of thunder. Therefore God says to his people that he is not looking for the carefully regimented sacrifice of animals but the spontaneous outpouring of passionate thanksgiving. That's the offering he's after. And this thanksgiving is not just a matter of words but deeds—actions that show our commitment to being faithful to his Word. "The life that pleases me," he says, "is a life lived in the gratitude of grace" (v. 23). Let's make this our lifestyle.

Make a list of all the things that you're thankful to God for today. Name and number them. Then enter his gates with thanksgiving in your heart.

A Passionate Faith

PSALMS 51-52

$\mathcal{O}$ne thing we learn from this translation of the Psalms is that God loves it when our hearts are passionate for him. He wants us to be on fire, not lukewarm or cold. Here in Psalm 51 we see David coming to the Lord in passionate repentance. This is no formulaic apology to God. This is true godly sorrow, occasioned by the consequences of David's adultery (2 Samuel 12). Notice how real and raw David's passion for forgiveness is here. He looks back on his sinful past with a shattered heart. But he also looks forward to his future restoration with overflowing hope, knowing that God will bless him and use him again. This is true repentance. Let's model ours on David's.

$\mathcal{D}$avid wrote Psalm 52 after he had been on the run from King Saul, facing taunts and threats from King Achish's men (1 Samuel 21:10-15). Just as David is passionate in his repentance in Psalm 51, so he is passionate in his decrees before God in Psalm 52. He declares that the big shots will be brought down. They have trusted in their wealth, not in the Lord. David, on the other hand, decrees that God will give him abundance because he has put his trust in the Lord, not in money and power. He decrees that he is a flourishing olive tree in the house of the Lord and that God's passion toward him is eternal. Let's make this same decree for our lives as we put our trust in God.

No matter your circumstances today, look beyond them to your Father. If life is bad, trust God to turn things around. If life is good, trust God still and not the blessings he has given you. Talk to your Father about how you trust him more than anything else today.

_____

_____

_____

_____

_____

_____

_____

_____

_____

_____

_____

_____

_____

_____

Withering and Flourishing

PSALMS 53–54

Every man or woman has a responsibility for his or her own soul care. The foolish person who denies God neglects their soul. The wise person who pursues the presence of God with relentless passion cares for their soul. In Psalm 53, David pours out his heart to God in a time of anguish about the number of people denying that God exists. Such people possess a "withering soul." "There's no God for me," they declare (v. 1). They fail to see the Lord looking down with tender eyes of love from heaven's balcony, searching among the sons and daughters of Adam for those whose souls are set on pleasing him. Such souls are wise. They are always turned in prayer toward heaven. Let's be wise and care for our souls.

The wise soul flourishes while the foolish soul withers. The foolish soul cares nothing about God. But the wise soul declares in the words of Psalm 54, "Lord, I will offer myself freely, and everything I am I give to you" (v. 6). Such a person flourishes because they are familiar with the dynamics of a divine encounter. They know the experience of having God lean into their heart, wrapping it around with his loving presence. For such a person, they may experience conflict and opposition on the outside, but on the inside they are at peace. They know that all is well with their soul because they worship God and see in advance the victory that is theirs. Let's cultivate our inner life by choosing to praise regardless of our circumstances.

Praying the Scriptures waters the soil of our hearts and prevents the godly things growing there from withering. Take portions of Psalms 53 and 54 and turn them into passionate prayer and praise.

The Place of Rest and Peace

PSALMS 55–56

There is a place of *Shabbat* and *shalom* in the presence of the Lord. Shabbat means "rest." Shalom means "peace." In Psalm 55, David is trembling because he is encircled by fearsome enemies. He wants to run away to a safe place. Then he realizes that there's a place he can access anytime in God's presence—the place of everlasting *Shabbat* and *shalom*. This is the higher place, a place secure from the raging storm of intimidation and oppression. This is his Shelter, the protective and majestic presence of "God-Enthroned" (v. 19). This is the place to which David moves his soul (v. 17), committing to run to it rather than away from his problems. Enter that place and hear God greet you with *Shabbat shalom!*

The place of rest and peace is accessed by the key of trust. In Psalm 56, David declares, "In the day that I'm afraid, I lay all my fears before you and trust in you with all my heart" (v. 3). In that posture, David knows that with God on his side, he is no longer afraid. And so worry gives way to worship—to the roaring praises of God. In this secret place of *Shabbat* and *shalom*, God sees David's tears and stores them in a bottle. He hears David call out to him for help as a child calls out to a father. He responds to David's thanksgiving in times of trouble and reveals that he is truly on David's side. What a glorious place of rest and peace this is! Let's make it our home, our daily dwelling place.

What are the things that you're tempted to run from right now?
Bring them in heartfelt prayer before the Lord. Run into the
arms of your Father instead, your true place of rest and peace.

_____

_____

_____

_____

_____

_____

_____

_____

_____

_____

_____

_____

_____

_____

Strengthening Yourself in the Lord: Part 1
PSALMS 57–58

David strengthened himself in the Lord during times of trouble. Psalms 57 and 58 are vivid examples of how David did this in practice, giving us abiding lessons to apply in our lives. In Psalm 57, David does this by making wise choices. The first choice he makes is to enter God's embrace. "I will hide," he cries (v. 1). The second is to pray with passion for his Father's help. "I will cry out," he declares (v. 2). The third choice he makes is to worship God. "I will thank you," he decrees (v. 9). These choices cause his heart to become quiet and confident and to sing with passion rather than moan with self-pity. These powerful choices transported David from a moment of weakness to a source of strength that turned around his circumstances.

One of the keys to strengthening yourself in the Lord is to remember that our God is a God of justice and that today's wrongs will be righted. This is one of the principal lessons of Psalm 58. David bemoans the corrupt justice and the lack of justice on the earth and the countless examples of evil seeming to triumph over good. But he then calls his soul to focus on the future rather than the present. Hope begins to overflow in his heart as he looks forward to the day when God will right every wrong, punish those who have rejected God and his ways, and reward the godly. From declaring in Psalm 57, "I will," he now declares in Psalm 58, "God will" (v. 9). Strengthen yourself in the Lord by remembering God's future.

Write down a list of choices that are designed to strengthen you in the Lord and which the Holy Spirit is urging you to make right now.

Strengthening Yourself in the Lord: Part 2

PSALMS 59–60

David strengthened himself in God whenever he felt depressed or oppressed. In Psalm 59 he gives us another lesson in how to do this. Once again he is feeling terrorized. This time he chooses to wait upon the Lord (v. 9). This waiting is not something passive in the Psalms. It is a conscious and intentional act of entwining yourself to God. This entwining process is activated through high praise; in other words, through focusing on God rather than on one's enemies. As David does this, his cry of desperation turns into a song of adoration—a song in which he celebrates three sublime truths. God is his Strength, his Stronghold, and his Savior. Let's do the same and be lifted up in the process to a high place where our lyrics of love fill the atmosphere.

When you draw near to your Father in prayer, do you find strangely encouraging thoughts pass through your mind? This is God speaking to you, just as we see in Psalm 60. David is impacted here by a sense of God's absence, not his presence. Rather than wallow in doubt, David contends for the presence of God. He presses in and cries out, "Come to your beloved ones" (v. 5). Then the sanctuary doors to God's presence spring open, and the Father begins to speak prophetically about the future of his people. These prophetic words not only release hope but they also awaken a heroic spirit in David (v. 12). Activating the prophetic strengthens and emboldens us.

Write a prayer asking the Father to help you hear his voice with greater clarity and activate the prophetic in your life with greater frequency.

_____

_____

_____

_____

_____

_____

_____

_____

_____

_____

_____

_____

_____

_____

_____

_____

_____

Strengthening Yourself in the Lord: Part 3
PSALMS 61–62

To what extent does your heart long for a revelation of the glory of God? David clearly had a great love for the presence of God's glory and the glory of God's presence. In Psalm 61 he shows us how God's glory is a key to strengthening yourself in the Lord. "When I'm feeble," he prays, "guide me into your glory" (v. 2). This glorious, manifest, powerful presence is "a paradise of protection" for David (v. 3). Dwelling under this "splendor-shadow," he is held firmly in God's wraparound presence (v. 4). This is a magnificent secret to strengthening yourself in the Lord. Seek the glory of God's presence. There you will be enthroned and treated like a king. You will no longer feel weak, but strong. You will no longer be helpless, but heroic.

In Psalm 62 we discover one of the great secrets of strengthening yourself in the Lord. It is the simple prayer, "More, Lord." The people who remain perpetually strong in God are those who rely on the power of God and who pursue the presence of God. They know that all the love they need is found in him. Therefore they stand perpetually before God, the One they love. They wait faithfully for God to manifest his glory, and they do this because they believe the promise: "The greater your passion for more— the greater reward I will give" (v. 12). Waiting, therefore, doesn't involve passivity. It involves passion. Always position yourself to cry, "More, Lord." The proud despise this place, but the humble camp there continually.

Spend some time applying the principle articulated in Psalm 62:12, expressing your passion for "more."

_____

_____

_____

_____

_____

_____

_____

_____

_____

_____

_____

_____

_____

_____

_____

_____

_____

Thirsting for God

PSALMS 63–64

*H*ave you ever been lovesick for God? One of the reasons why God regarded David as a man after his own heart was because David couldn't stand the thought of being apart from God's presence. David pined for the presence of God in Psalm 63. Every believer goes through experiences like David, when they feel like they're in a weary wilderness and God is distant. The key when this happens is to stir up a greater yearning for God and to seek his presence, power, and glory. When we are in the desert, this is no time for passivity. We must passionately pursue God with Davidic zeal, knowing that the anointing of his presence is the one thing that will satisfy our thirst.

*S*ometimes the desert experience involves isolation and condemnation. We are all alone and feel that others are out to slander, accuse, and destroy us. This was David's experience in Psalm 64. He was keenly conscious of the people who had formed unholy alliances in order to trap him. Their words against him were like poison-tipped arrows. David comes before God, trusting in divine vindication. God has his own arrows, and he will sooner or later use them against David's oppressors. Therefore David makes a decree: the lovers of God will rejoice because they find their peace in the wraparound presence of God. How wonderful it is to place our trust in God, who will come to our rescue!

"The anointing of your presence satisfies me like nothing else"
(Psalm 63:5). Write a prayer confessing your longing, yearning,
and desperation for more of the anointing of God's presence.

The Healing of the Land

PSALMS 65-66

*H*ave you ever seen the connection between revivals and the healing of the land? When God visits the earth with his manifest presence, these revival seasons don't just transform individuals and communities; they heal rivers and oceans! This is one of the most beautiful truths declared by David in Psalm 65. "Your visitations of glory bless the earth," he sings (v. 9). When God visits us in power, there are richer harvests, cleaner rivers, more luxuriant fields, and more fertile valleys. Even creation breaks into song when God Almighty revives his people and heals the land (2 Chronicles 7:14). Many throughout the world cry out for the protection of nature, and our Father's presence is the answer.

*W*hen God visits his people in revival, there's no way you can stop them pouring out their hearts in passionate thanksgiving. That's what Psalm 66 is—an explosion of thanksgiving for God's miracle-working power on the earth. As people see the mighty miracles that God does, they are filled with awe. It takes their breath away. When God rescued the Israelites from the Egyptians, he parted the Red Sea. Even the sea was involved in the dramatic deliverance of his people. Such signs cause the whole earth to wonder. So David invites everyone, everywhere, to tune their songs to his glory. God's glorious visitations cause all the earth to sing. So let's join in the song every day!

God promises that if we seek him with all our hearts, he will heal our land. Write a prayer receiving mercy over your life and releasing mercy over your community, and ask him to heal the environment where you live.

_____

_____

_____

_____

_____

_____

_____

_____

_____

_____

_____

_____

_____

_____

Blessing the Nations

It's important to remember that God blesses us in order to bless the world. Those who only pray, "Bless me, God," miss the point. What's radical in Psalm 67 is how David connects the nations coming to know God to God blessing us. We should forget neither God's desire to bless us nor the nations that have yet to taste his blessing, but instead remember the power of our blessing is that it testifies his heart to the nations so that they may be saved. Let's embrace a mind-set that says, "Bless me at your fountain, O God, so that I may go to the nations and bless them," and, "How glad the nations will be when you are their king!"

What does true mission look like? Is it just a matter of words—preaching a message? Or is it more than that? According to Psalm 68:11, "God Almighty declares the word of the gospel with power." There are, therefore, at least two things we need as we seek to bless the nations: words (the gospel) and wonders (power). But there's a third. David tells us that God is a Father to the fatherless and a Champion Friend to the widow. He sets the lonely in families and causes the prisoners to rejoice. This is who God is in his holy place. If that is so, then we must add a third dimension to our mission: works! Words, works, and wonders—let's be three-dimensional in blessing the nations.

One nation specifically mentioned in these Psalms is Africa. "Africa will send her noble envoys to you, O God. They will come running, stretching out their hands in love to you" (Psalm 68:31). Bless Africa today and claim that beautiful promise in prayer.

_____

_____

_____

_____

_____

_____

_____

_____

_____

_____

_____

_____

_____

_____

_____

Christ's Passion and Ours

PSALMS 69-70

Along with Psalm 22, Psalm 69 contains some of the most outstanding prophetic glimpses of the passion of Christ in the book of Psalms. Lamenting his own sufferings, David catches glimpses of the future agonies of the crucified Messiah, Jesus Christ. At times in this psalm, it could almost be Jesus crying out in thirst, exhaustion, tears, and torment. David is mocked, cursed, and disgraced. He says that passion for God's house consumes him (just as Jesus said). The only respite he receives is when his tormenters offer him vinegar for his thirst (just as they did for Jesus). Let's always show our passionate appreciation for Christ's passion.

There are two ways in which the word *passion* can be understood. The first refers to a heart on fire. The second refers to the sufferings of Christ (from the Latin *patiens*, meaning "suffering"). In Psalm 69 we looked at the passion of Christ (i.e. his sufferings). In Psalm 70 we are challenged to have hearts on fire in our relationship with God. Those who worship God are invited to be lovers of God, continually rejoicing in God their Savior. In the original Hebrew language, the word *savior* contains the root word *Yeshua*, the name Jesus was given. Let's be lovers of God and rejoice in a passionate way for all that *Yeshua* has done for us.

Go through Psalm 69 and extract all the phrases and verses that point to the cross. Then turn those into heartfelt prayers of thanksgiving.

_____

_____

_____

_____

_____

_____

_____

_____

_____

_____

_____

_____

_____

_____

_____

_____

_____

_____

Singing in Old Age

PSALMS 71–72

Someone once said, "You're never too old to be bold." In Psalm 71, called here "The Psalm of Old Age," we see how true that is. The singer of this song is an elderly man. As he looks back over his past, he declares that he has held on to God all the days of his life, trusting in the Lord. God has continually helped him in life's journey. Now his prayer is that God would strengthen him and stay close. He vows that he will tell the next generation of the great signs and wonders God has done. He prays for passionate excitement in the telling of these stories. His decree is that God will revive them again. What an example this old man is!

If Psalm 71 shows us an old man vowing to tell the next generation about God's supernatural power, Psalm 72 shows us a father praying for blessings upon his son. This song in fact is a prayer of King David for his son and successor, King Solomon. David prays for his son to have "the gift of justice" (v. 1) so that "the poor and humble will have an advocate with the king" (v. 4). He prays that his son will exercise his authority to rule and extend his dominion from sea to sea. David prophecies that kings will bring tributes to his son's throne and the humble and helpless will know his son's kindness. What a fine example of how to bless the next generation through prayer and prophecy.

There are few things more beautiful than an old person with a youthful passion for God. Pray for those you know who are old in the faith. If you are of old age, ask God to give you a new excitement in sharing your testimony and interceding prophetically for the next generation.

You're All I Need

PSALMS 73-74

Have you ever had an encounter with God that radically altered your perspective? The writer of Psalm 73 clearly did. He found himself bemoaning the injustices of the world. On the one hand, ungodly people were enjoying greater and greater prosperity. On the other, God's people were enduring daily hardship. What's fair in that? Then one day the writer had an encounter with the glory of God. In an instant, his distorted perspective vanished. He suddenly understood that it is better to have God's strong and glorious presence anointing and protecting you than all the wealth in the world. The former is permanent and the latter transient. As a result of his encounter, he cried, "Forever you're all I need" (v. 26). Let that cry be ours today and every day.

God's visitation always occurs within the context of our desperation. When God's people cry, "You're all I need," the Holy Spirit is irresistibly drawn to the sound of our desperation. This is very much the theme of Psalm 74. In a time of great distress, the composer sings a song of passionate pleading for God to "wrap us back into your heart again" (v. 2). In the place of devastation, the writer expresses his longing for God. "Come running to bring your restoring grace to these ruins," he cries (v. 3). What a phrase that is—restoring grace! Maybe you feel like your life is in shambles right now. Cry out to God, "You're forever all I need." Ask for his restoring grace so that you might rebuild a godly life amidst the rubble.

Take that phrase, "You're all I need," and turn it now
into a prayer or a song of worship to God.

_____

_____

_____

_____

_____

_____

_____

_____

_____

_____

_____

_____

_____

_____

_____

The Fearsome One

PSALMS 75–76

Someone once said that there are many who fear God, some who love God, but very few who both love and fear the Lord. Psalms 75 and 76 are praise songs to the God who must be feared as well as loved. On the one hand, in Psalm 75 the songwriter proclaims that God is the "Near One" (v. 1). He is the one who draws near to those who draw near to him. In that proximity we find intimacy. At the same time, however, this same loving God is the one who, when the time is ripe, will judge the world with perfect righteousness. This same God who embraces us with affection also says that he is going to shake the earth. Behold God today as both loving and fearsome.

As soon as we start talking about fearing the Lord, some are turned off. "All this talk of the fear of the Lord is toxic," they say. But the biblical idea of fearing God does not mean a cowering, miserable submission to a divine terrorist. It means being so filled with awe at the majestic otherness and radiant holiness of God that we long to do his will and please his heart. This is very much the stance taken by the songwriter in Psalm 76. His heart is full of passionate praise for the resplendent majesty and incomparable glory of the Living God. This God roars his rebuke, felling and stunning his enemies. This God is greatly to be feared. We ought to hold our breath in awe of him. He is not just the Near One. He is the Awesome One.

Does your worship focus more on awe of God or affection for God? Draw near to your Father today and allow him to reveal himself to you in that radical middle between awe and affection.

The Spirit and the Word

Like you and me, God frequents the places where he is wanted. This is why revival is most likely to come among those who are desperate for more of God's Spirit. In Psalm 77, the songwriter utters a heartfelt, lyrical cry for more of the Holy Spirit. He stretches out his hands to heaven. He pleads for God's comforting grace. He longs for more of the presence of God. He remembers the wonders and signs that the Mighty One performed in Israel's history. He complains that he no longer sees the miracle-working power of God at work. He pines and aches for a fresh revelation of God's manifest presence. He is desperate for God's glory bursts to come again. What an example this songwriter is! May our Father reveal himself to you today in such a way that you would desire him like David did.

Revivals occur when people start to venerate the written Word of God, the Bible. In Psalm 78, the songwriter exalts the Torah, the Father's written Word (i.e. the Law). He celebrates and promotes "a living faith in the laws of life" (v. 7), vowing that he will tell the next generation the Torah tales of God's mighty miracles. He then retells the story of the Israelites' great escape from Egypt, showing how they were protected and blessed when they trusted in God's promises, and how they found themselves in trouble when they were forgetful of the Word. He exalts the True God of covenant, the God who keeps his promises by performing epic signs and marvels. If we want to see revival, we must believe in God's Word and long for his Spirit.

Love the Word, which is a light to your path, and welcome the Spirit, the fire of God's love. Invite your Father to give you a greater longing for his Spirit and a greater faith in his Word and his promises.

Revive Us, O God!

PSALM 79-80

One of the abiding lessons of revival history is this: great awakenings occur when a few men and women get on their knees and plead with God. Psalm 79 is such a prayer. The writer is living through a time of national devastation. God's city is in ruins, and his people are in despair. A national disaster of seismic proportions is taking place. In the midst of the rubble, one man gets praying. He cries out to the God of the Breakthrough to come and forgive and heal his people. His passionate prayer is this: "Demonstrate your glory-power" (v. 11). See here how desperation leads to intercession and intercession to visitation. This is the divine pattern. May we submit to it again that we may see God's glory-power come.

In Psalm 80, the songwriter cries out to God, "Revive us again" (v. 18). God's holy lovers burn to see God shine forth from his radiant throne of light. They cry out to see the beaming face of the Lover shine forth upon their lovesick souls. They offer their tears by the bowlful to God and pray, "Come back, come back, O God, and restore us!" (v. 7). They ask God to look down from heaven and see the crisis of his people. They implore God to reveal the Branch-Man, the Messiah, to them. Their hearts are set on seeing a revelation of the Son of God, Jesus Christ, in the nation. Let's pray passionately for a fresh manifestation and glorification of Jesus in our time.

Ask in desperation for God to reveal greater measures of his goodness to you.
Spend some time crying, "revive us, O God."

_____

_____

_____

_____

_____

_____

_____

_____

_____

_____

_____

_____

_____

_____

_____

_____

Authentic Celebration

Singing God's praises in the midst of a crowd of God-lovers is one of the most exhilarating experiences a human being can have. Here in Psalm 81 the writer explores the dynamics of praise. Just singing about God makes a person strong. Shouting for joy to God our Champion is what we were created to do. When that's led by a band comprising of percussion, stringed instruments, and wind instruments, then the joy really begins to arise. God loves hearing this kind of high praise from us. As long as we remember all that he has done for us and have grateful, obedient hearts, such festivals of joy will cause us to feast on revelation truth, dripping like honey from the cliff tops of heaven. It's time for us all to join with the psalmist and say, "I'll keep shouting," and "I will sing" (vv. 1–2).

There are many whose passion is to buy the latest worship music and sing songs of praise, both in private and in public. There are some who love to feed the hungry, clothe the naked, care for the orphan, and defend the widow. There are few who love to do both—to worship God with great passion and serve the poor with deep compassion. This is why it is so important to set Psalm 82 alongside Psalm 81. Here we enter the courtroom of heaven. "All rise" is the cry as the Judge of all the earth enters (v. 1). His charge against the judges of the earth is that they have forgotten true justice, which is to defend those who are defenseless—to champion the fatherless and the forgotten. What a thing it would be if the church could reunite celebration and compassion, worship and justice!

What can you do to unite worship and compassion—singing and service?
Ask the Holy Spirit to show you how he wants you to respond.

_____

_____

_____

_____

_____

_____

_____

_____

_____

_____

_____

_____

_____

_____

_____

_____

_____

_____

Learning to Dig Deep

PSALMS 83-84

What do you do when you're experiencing a season of personal or national trouble? In Psalms 83 and 84, we find some answers. In Psalm 83, Israel is surrounded by enemies who have become stirred in uproar. They are fuelled by a dark lust to see Israel wiped off the map. They want to change the history books and erase every memory of her. In the midst of this terrifying ordeal the psalmist digs deep into the past. He remembers those times when God blew away Israel's enemies. "Repeat history, O God" is his cry (v. 11). The psalmist's longing is not that these hostile nations will be obliterated (which is what they desired for Israel). It is that they will see God's greatness and acknowledge that Yahweh alone is Lord. Sometimes our future testimony is dependent on us remembering past history.

Have you ever traveled through the dark valley of tears? If you have, Psalm 84 is for you. In this magnificent song, the psalmist gives voice to that lovesick longing for God that comes when we experience testing times of pain. He knows that dwelling close to the presence of God is his strength. His call to us is "dig deep" when your path winds through the valley of tears (v. 6). Don't let the pain become your preoccupation. Make it your priority to dig deep until you find that secret brook of blessing filled by the rain of revival outpourings. Then you will grow stronger with every step forward, because just one day of intimacy in God's presence is like a thousand days of joy rolled into one. In times of trouble, let's dig deep—deep into the past (Psalm 83) and deep into the presence (Psalm 84).

What would it mean for you to dig deep?

Turn those thoughts into passionate prayer and specific action.

_____

_____

_____

_____

_____

_____

_____

_____

_____

_____

_____

_____

_____

_____

_____

_____

_____

_____

_____

The Fountain of Grace

PSALMS 85–86

*M*any people are resistant to the idea of God's anger. But Psalm 85 does not shy away from this aspect of God's nature. In the psalm, God's people have been experiencing deep conviction over their sins. They have been on the receiving end of God's wrath—his measured, loving, and justified anger with sin, wickedness, and injustice. Having repented, they are now enjoying mercy. Impacted by divine kindness and mercy, the psalmist prays, "Revive us again, O God" and, "Give us a fresh start" (v. 6). What a great and glorious thing it is to know that the fire of God's wrath is extinguished by the sweet spring rain of his mercy. When we repent, his power and presence shine over all his lovers, his glory hovers over us.

*S*ometimes we are called to corporate repentance. At other times we are led to repent of our sins in private. If Psalm 85 describes corporate repentance, Psalm 86 portrays one man—King David—experiencing personal and profound contrition. In a moment of gut-wrenching brokenness, David cries out to God in desperation, "Bring me to your fountain of grace" (v. 3). David cries tears of repentance, but he prays for God to restore his joy. He makes his confession of faith: "Your grace fountain keeps overflowing, drenching all your lovers who pray to you" (v. 5). For us today, this grace fountain is the cross. It's the blood of Jesus that causes God's grace to cover our sins when we repent. When we experience this overwhelming reality, the right thing to do is to thank God. The greater our gratitude, the greater the release of grace will be.

"Bring me to your grace fountain."

Turn this phrase into your own prayer of passionate longing.

_____

_____

_____

_____

_____

_____

_____

_____

_____

_____

_____

_____

_____

_____

_____

_____

_____

_____

Christ the King

*A*re you overwhelmed at times by the trouble and conflict throughout the world? If you are, Psalm 87 will give you great reassurance. This is a passionate song in praise of God's love for Zion, his holy city. The word *Zion* is used more than 150 times in the Bible. It refers to the city of David and to the people of Israel (Isaiah 60:14). Many things are said in praise of Zion here, but chief among them is that it is here that the Mighty Man was born. Out of the people of Israel, Jesus Christ the anointed King grew up. One day, the psalmist prophesies, people from the nations of the earth will acknowledge this. They will truly acknowledge God and his Son, Jesus Christ. So if you're tempted to be disturbed by world events, remember that all nations will acknowledge Israel's God and his Son, Christ the Mighty King.

*W*hen we think of Christ the King, we must never forget that he chose to reveal himself as the suffering Servant King. He did not come as a triumphant, militaristic king. Psalm 88 is a vivid reminder of this. As you read it, imagine Christ on the cross speaking these words. They go deep into the heart of Christ's sense of abandonment by his Father at Calvary. In his human heart, Christ's life is ebbing from him as spectators consider him pierced and abandoned. Christ feels the heavy weight of his Father's wrath over sin. All his friends have deserted him. His arms are opened wide as he hangs upon the cross, humiliated and broken. In his first coming, Christ revealed himself as the Suffering King. In his second coming, he will return as the Conquering King.

How different Christ is from the kings of the earth!

Spend time in passionate praise of Christ, the Returning King of all the earth.

Our Mortality, God's Immortality

PSALMS 89-90

*H*ave you ever been overwhelmed by a sense of your own mortality? This is one of the insights of Psalm 89, a song made up of four stanzas. In the first the psalmist praises the infinite majesty and faithfulness of God. In the second he praises God for the way he makes and keeps his covenant promises. In the third the note changes, and he confesses he feels forsaken and defeated. In the fourth he confronts his mortality, acknowledging that he is nothing but dust, here today and gone tomorrow. In the end he returns to where he began, with high praise of God, blessing him for his faithfulness. When we experience a sense of our mortality, let's praise God that he is everlasting and so are his promises to us.

*P*salm 90 is a beautiful song in praise of God's eternal nature. The psalmist is painfully aware that all human beings will one day be swept away into the sleep of death. Our days soon become years, and then our lifetime comes to an end. On the other hand, God is not bound by time or restricted by mortality. He has been from everlasting to everlasting. One thousand years pass before God's eyes like a yesterday that has quickly faded. While we live for seventy years, more if God gives the grace for it, God lives forever. So the psalmist asks God to help him to number his days and to respond to his correction while there is still time. In the end, our lives are but a dream, so the songwriter (said to be Moses here) asks that God would fill our hearts with songs of joy to the end of our days. Make that your prayer too.

Praise God that he lives forever and that his promises are everlasting and true. Share any fears you have about your own mortality, but give God praise that one day he will give his faithful children the gift of immortality when Christ returns.

_____

_____

_____

_____

_____

_____

_____

_____

_____

_____

_____

_____

_____

_____

_____

The Protected Life

PSALMS 91–92

While life on earth has many profound challenges and perplexing mysteries, God's lovers are destined to live under the covering of God's protection. Psalm 91 is a magnificent praise song about God's protective love. His massive arms are wrapped perpetually around us, shielding us from demonic attacks by day and by night. Even in a time of national disaster, thousands may be killed but we will remain unharmed. God sends his angels with special orders to protect us wherever we go. As God's royal lovers, we live our lives within the protective shadow of God Most High. We find and feel his presence even when we are greatly under pressure. We enjoy a feast that perpetually satisfies because God is our glorious Hero. Let's hide our lives in God, our secret Hiding Place.

The protected life is not the privilege given to anyone but only to those who are lovers of God. Such lovers, according to Psalm 92, wake up every morning and thank God for his kindness and go to bed every night proclaiming that God is faithful. Such lovers overflow with worship all the time. They are happy lovers who simply can't contain their gladness. They know what it is to be anointed with the fresh oil of God's Holy Spirit. They feel empowered for a victorious life. Those who lie in wait to defeat them are themselves defeated. God's lovers, meanwhile, flourish like palm trees in the courtyards of heaven, growing from strength to strength and from victory to victory. Even in old age they remain fresh and fruitful under the anointing. Let's thrive, not just survive, in God. Let's remain in his protective love.

Here's a great promise to turn into praise. "Because you have delighted in me as a great lover, I will greatly protect you. I will set you in a high place, safe and secure before my face" (Psalm 91:14).

Lovers of Righteousness

PSALMS 93–94

What a magnificent example of high praise Psalm 93 is! Here David composes a song in which he expresses his appreciation of God's majesty. God reigns over all the earth. His sovereignty is on display as he sits on his throne, in charge of the entire earth. Even at the dawn of creation, the waves rose up in chaos, but God's majestic power stilled them—just as they were stilled when Jesus rebuked them in his earthly ministry. This God reigns from his palace in heaven—a palace adorned by the beauty of holiness. Holiness is the environment in which God dwells. It is the atmosphere in which he reveals his miracle-working power. Those who want to see demonstrations of God's sovereign power must create environments where holiness is evident. Allow God to decorate the interior of your heart and home with the beauty of his holiness.

The world is a wicked place where evil men and women do despicable things. What will it take for such people, who even murder widows and orphaned children, to come to repentance? Psalm 94 tells us. It is when God's lovers are lovers of righteousness that the tide will turn. It is when those of us who praise God with our mouths have hearts that are holy that the perpetrators of injustice will be convicted. Lovers of righteousness are the answer. Through them, God will pour out the irresistible radiance of his revelation light, searing the consciences of those who commit injustice and persecute God's lovers. Then their proud taunts that God is deaf and blind will be proven wrong. They will know that God hears and sees everything. It's time for us to become lovers of righteousness.

Commit yourself to God's Word and ways afresh, and ask the
Holy Spirit to reveal any areas of your heart and home that are
not currently adorned with the beauty of God's holiness.

Ecstatic Praise

PSALMS 95-96

*H*ave you ever been lost in wonder as you have praised God? In Psalm 95 the songwriter shows us what it is to give everything in worship to God. He exhorts us to sing to the Lord and to utter loud shouts of praise. He tells us not to hold back but to give God our all. He encourages us to kneel before the Creator God and to bow before the Majestic Maker. Since we are his lovers, we are to listen to his voice, to yield our hearts to him in full surrender so that we never become hard-hearted and stubborn like the Israelites at Meribah and Massah. See how the psalmist urges us to yield the whole of our being to God—our voices, knees, ears, and hearts. Let's adore him with our bodies, souls, and spirits, so that everything within us is responding to the call to praise.

*T*he key to ecstatic worship is the full surrender of our spirits to God Almighty. When we yield our spirits to the Spirit of the Lord in the abandonment of love, then we experience the euphoria of singing a new song from a burning heart. This is very much the call in Psalm 96. The psalmist here urges everyone to surrender to Yahweh. Every person on the planet, every people group in the world, is invited to confess that Jehovah alone deserves all the honor and the glory. This invitation is then given to the skies and the earth, to the oceans and the fields. This shows that ecstatic praise (v. 12) is not only activated when everything within us worships God, but it is also activated when every nation and every part of creation lifts up joyous songs of praise to their Maker. Let's do our part by responding to the invitation personally.

Give God praise with the whole of your being, and experience a foretaste of that day when people from every tribe and nation will praise him.

_____

_____

_____

_____

_____

_____

_____

_____

_____

_____

_____

_____

_____

_____

_____

_____

_____

_____

When God's Glory Falls

PSALMS 97-98

*T*he writer of Psalm 97 is consumed with the revelation of God's righteousness. He sees it so clearly, and really, he sees our God so clearly, that he laughs at the idea of anyone worshiping an idol they crafted with their own hands. It's as though he says, "Really? You have worshiped what your own hands made? You will feel ashamed when you see the real God." This is what births true worship—a true revelation of God himself. No obligation, no laws, no list of rules can produce the true fear of the Lord in our hearts that produces genuine worship. Only a revelation of God himself produces such abandon. What a blessing that this revelation also teaches us righteousness in a way that all our efforts to obey laws have failed to do. Will you seek a true revelation of God in his righteousness today?

*O*ne characteristic of authentic revival is uninhibited praise to God. David once declared that he could be even more undignified than he had been when he danced nakedly before God in public worship. Now in Psalm 98 he gives us a vivid portrait of what revived worship looks like. As people begin to see God's miracles and marvels, they break out of their religious boxes and cut loose with passionate praise. New songs are sung and written in adoration of God and his Son, Jesus Christ. The people of God make melody as never before. There is a newfound unity and harmony in people's worship as everyone in unison shouts out, "Glory to the Lord!" (v. 7). As wave upon wave of the Holy Spirit breaks upon communities, people declare, "Look! Here he comes!" (v. 9). Let's open our hearts afresh and abandon ourselves to waves of God's Spirit.

Psalm 97 says that God sows seeds of light within his lovers, releasing a harvest of righteousness. Welcome seeds of light into your heart and pray for a great harvest of righteousness.

Weeping and Laughing

PSALMS 99–100

$\mathcal{S}$ome people only want an intellectual faith. But in making that preference, they forget that God made us with emotions and that these (and not just our minds) are to be engaged in the way we relate to him. In Psalm 99, the psalmist urges us to recognize the holiness of God and to worship him in awe. "Let everyone praise this breathtaking God," he cries, "for he is holy" (v. 3). This is particularly important when God's people have gone astray in promoting a theology that only stresses God's intimacy but neglects God's purity. When that happens we inevitably experience times of crisis, and the only antidote is for praying priests (that's all of us) to cry out in travailing intercession. Facedown before his glory throne, we find that he is the great Forgiver. Let's make room for weeping before the Lord as we worship him facedown.

$\mathcal{H}$ave you ever been so filled with the joy of the Lord that you couldn't stop laughing? God loves it when large gatherings of people give him shouts of joy, as in Psalm 100. When we bring him the gift of laughter and serve him with gladness, he rejoices too because we are the people of his pleasure. When we rejoice, it shows that our affections and not just our intellects have become engaged with him. If we need any reasons for rejoicing in the Lord, then the psalmist gives us some: we have a lot to thank him for, not the least of which are his welcoming goodness, his amazing love, and his astounding kindness. And if we still need a reason, the song ends in praise of God's faithfulness to his promises throughout all generations. Let's engage our emotions in worship and "affectionately bless his beautiful name" (v. 4).

Have you ever soaked the carpet with your tears as you cried out
to God facedown, or brought the gift of holy laughter to him in praise?
Ask God to activate your affection for him in weeping and laughing.

I Need Your Help

PSALMS 101–102

What is the spiritual atmosphere like in your home? In Psalm 101, David says to God, "I need your help" (v. 2). The context is his home. "I'm trying my best to walk the way of integrity, especially in my own home," he cries (v. 2). It's obviously been a great challenge. He makes a commitment to guard his eyes and not gaze upon anything vulgar, anything that draws his heart away from God. He resolves to have an inner circle of friends who are lovers of God and only to allow these people of purity in his house. He dedicates himself to waking up every morning with a passion for doing the right thing. His prayer above all is for the Lord to appear in his home, for a manifestation of God's presence in his house. What a wonderful prayer for all of us to pray with regard to our homes.

If the prayer for help in Psalm 101 is prayed in the security and serenity of the writer's home, the one prayed in Psalm 102 is uttered in the day of distress. The writer's days of happiness have gone. He has lost his health, and his appetite is withering away with a raging fever. He is depressed and lonely, unable to sleep. "My crying fills my cup with salty tears" (v. 10). Then suddenly the note changes: "But then I remember that you, O Lord, still sit enthroned as King over all!" (v. 12). He appeals to God's mercy and his promises. God responds to the prayer of the broken and hears the cry of the homeless, he says. Remembering all this, he declares, "I cry out to you, my God, the Father of eternity" (v. 24). Whatever our situation, whether we have a home or are homeless, we can always say to God, "I need your help," and be sure that he hears.

The Holy Spirit is inviting you to make changes in your home.
What are they? Call out to the Father, "I need your help."

_____

_____

_____

_____

_____

_____

_____

_____

_____

_____

_____

_____

_____

_____

_____

The Father's Love

PSALMS 103-104

There is no love in the universe as strong, affectionate, holy and true as our Heavenly Father's love. Psalm 103 describes a Father who kisses our hearts with forgiveness, heals us inside and out, rescues us from hell, crowns us as kings, satisfies our desires with good things, and supercharges our life so that we can soar again like eagles. This is a Father who is unrelentingly kind to those who don't deserve it and unceasingly patient to those who fail him. David cries: "The same way a loving father feels toward his children; that's but a sample of your tender feelings toward us, your beloved children" (v. 13). The Father's loyal love is always available to those who bow facedown in awe of him. Let's give thanks now and every day for the Father's extravagant love.

The compassionate love of our heavenly Father is the theme of Psalm 104. In spite of the fact that God is the Creator, dwelling in shimmering light, he stoops down from heaven out of great compassion and kindness to look after all that he has made. Notice here the two aspects of the Father's nature. On the one hand he is transcendent, above and beyond his creation, dwelling in dazzling light. On the other he is immanent, involved with the making and maintenance of everything, from the stars and the planets to the oceans and the mountains. Our God is truly earth's Overseer. He has the power to make the earth tremble, but he chooses to draw near and feed the animals from his open hands. All this comes from his kindness and compassion. Let's always give thanks that the Father does not stay in heaven but is Immanuel, God with us.

God is a loving Father who is extravagantly kind and tenderhearted to those who don't deserve it. Turn this thought into passionate praise.

_____

_____

_____

_____

_____

_____

_____

_____

_____

_____

_____

_____

_____

_____

_____

_____

_____

_____

The Faithful Father

PSALMS 105–106

*M*any people have been fathered by someone who didn't keep his promises. This is tragic and causes children to doubt their father's words. Psalm 105 says our Father is true to his word. He made promises to Abraham, Isaac, and Jacob, and he has kept all of them. Even though the Hebrew people were originally nomadic and few, eventually they entered the land of promise and became numerous and abundant. Even when they found themselves enslaved for a time in Egypt, the Father remembered his promises and brought them out of servitude through his servant Moses, performing signs and wonders as he set the captives free. When they left they were laden with the gold and silver of Egypt! This is a Father who keeps his promises. Let the whole world shout, "Hallelujah!"

*H*ow many of us know that while our Father is always faithful, we are sometimes not? This great gap between our Father's faithfulness and our unfaithfulness is the theme of Psalm 106. Looking back at Israel's history, the Psalmist remembers how rebellious his ancestors were. This doesn't cause him to gloat. It brings him to tears. "We're just like them," is his cry. Every time God intervened in the story of Israel's escape from Egypt, it wasn't long before his people forgot what he had done. "How quickly they forgot your miracles of power" (v. 13). How quickly we do too. Every time we have rebelled, God has watched and waited like a patient dad, longing for us to cry out to him. Every time we do, he remembers his covenant promises and reveals his limitless love. God is truly a faithful dad. Let the whole world shout, "Hallelujah!"

Celebrate God's promise-keeping love today. Consider an area in which you find the most difficulty remaining faithful. Ask the Holy Spirit to reveal his faithfulness to you in such a way that it transforms this area of your life.

_____

_____

_____

_____

_____

_____

_____

_____

_____

_____

_____

_____

_____

_____

_____

_____

Let the World Know!

PSALMS 107–108

If we have a Father in heaven whose love is so constant and compassionate, then this news is far too good to keep to ourselves. That's the theme of Psalm 107. The song begins with the stirring thought that this God is "better than anyone could ever imagine" (v. 1). The God of the Bible is endlessly compassionate and kind, loving us like no earthly father ever could. Even when we foolishly rebel, he comes running when we call for help. The stories of his marvelous kindness and miracles of mercy are countless. Let's turn our own stories of the Father's love into songs of joy. Let's fill the charts and the airwaves with these creative songs. Let's know God's goodness deeply in our lives, then let us tell the world how good our God really is.

The songwriter says in Psalm 108, "I will awaken the dawn with my worship" (v. 2). Too often we rely on someone else to ignite a spirit of praise in our hearts when we have the freedom to make this choice for ourselves. We might not always be in the mood to worship, but drawing near to our Father will always give us fresh inspiration. Practice worship as a choice of your will, and you will find that his presence catches you up and changes your heart with his joy. As the psalmist says, "All the nations will hear my praise songs to you. Your love is so extravagant" (vv. 3–4). The songwriter's passion is for the world to see God's shining glory above the earth. Let that be our passion too. It's time to let the world know. "This is our story, this is our song!"

When have you been so excited about great news that you felt like you were bursting to tell everyone? That's the kind of passion the Father will inspire in us. Ask him to ignite an unquenchable flame of intensity and creativity to tell others our news of his love.

_____

_____

_____

_____

_____

_____

_____

_____

_____

_____

_____

_____

_____

_____

I Am Prayer

PSALMS 109–110

*W*hat is your pattern of prayer? Some people pray at a set time every day, maybe first thing in the morning. Other people don't have a set time but pray when they feel led. In Psalm 109, David makes an extraordinary statement: "I will pray until I become prayer itself" (v. 4). In the original Hebrew version of this psalm, David says, "I am prayer." One of the noblest ambitions of a lover of God is to become prayer. This was David's dream and he fulfilled it. His heart was constantly conversing with the Father, by day and by night. This conversation was not religious or formal—it was real and raw. In Psalm 109 it is especially real and raw. However much we may feel uneasy at times by the things David prays, what his words reveal is that the heart of prayer is the prayer of the heart. Let's not say prayers. Let's become prayer—real prayer!

*H*eartfelt prayer is a gateway into the courts of heaven. Never forget that you and I are the adopted sons and daughters of the High King of heaven. We are, by God's grace, kings and lords. When we start to pray in the Spirit, heaven's door opens and we are shown glorious things in the throne room of God. This was David's experience in Psalm 110, the Old Testament passage most quoted by the New Testament authors. In the spirit of prayer, David sees the Father and the Son in heaven (Jehovah God and the Lord Messiah), and he hears the Father telling his Son that all enemies will one day be under his footstool. David calls the Messiah, "Adonai," which means "Lord of Lords." We are the lords over whom Jesus is Lord! As we grow in prayer, we see more and more who Christ is, and we catch a glimpse of who we are in Christ as well.

The Father loves it when we converse with him naturally, honestly, and passionately. In what ways could you become more raw and real in prayer?

Delighting in the Lord
PSALMS 111–112

When someone is in love, it can safely be said that everything about the person they love brings them delight. They take pleasure in all they see and hear. It pleases them. This kind of delight is something that the Holy Spirit wants to stir up in us. In Psalm 111, the songwriter expresses his adoration of God as a passionate lover. He looks at what God has done in history (both his own and his nation's), and he absolutely revels in it. There is no religious indifference here. This is the delight of love. He looks with awe at the wonders of God and describes them as "delightfully mysterious" (v. 2). There is such a holy, supernatural genius to what God does that it leaves people astounded. Like a true lover, the psalmist declares, "Everything he does is full of splendor and beauty!" (v. 3). Let's position ourselves to take greater delight in our delightful God.

There are some promises in the Bible that are just so good, we all ought to take hold of them and believe them right away. Psalm 112 begins with one of the greatest of all: *everyone who delights in the Lord will be blessed beyond all expectation!* Do you want to be blessed beyond anything you could imagine or expect? Then delight yourself in the Lord. Take great pleasure in who he is and what he does. When you truly start to take pleasure in the pleasures of God, you will be blessed with influence, prosperity, and favor. Great wealth will fill your house, and life will be good for you. As you give to those in need, turning prosperity into charity, you will be utterly secure, steady and strong in all circumstances. As lovers of God, let's be moved by the fire of the Spirit to take great delight in the Lord and claim this outstanding promise.

When was the last time you truly took delight in the Lord?
Stir up your heart today to take greater delight in the Lover of your soul.

The God Who Draws Near

PSALMS 113-114

One of the most beautiful things about the King of the universe is that he does not remain aloof in his palace but draws near to his people and especially to those in need. In Psalm 113, the songwriter gives praise that God rules over the nations and that he is not remote but relational. God steps down to promote the poor and rescue the wretched. He provides the barren ones with children, turning childless couples into happy parents. He turns paupers into princes, giving them thrones to replace their cardboard shelters. What a kind King this is! Our God reigns over all things, and yet he enters the poverty and agony of our world. The King enters our mess and our misery so that we who are poor might become rich and we who are full of shame might become crowned with honor. Let's always give passionate praise for the King of kindness.

One of the unique revelations of the Judeo-Christian faith is this: that the God who reigns over all the earth is not the God above us or the God against us but the God among us! Psalm 114 gives voice to this great truth in lyrical adoration. Here the songwriter celebrates the epic marvel of the Exodus—the great escape of God's people from Egypt. What did the God of the Universe do? He stepped down from heaven and caused the earth to tremble at his presence. He parted the Red Sea and the River Jordan too. Why did he do this? He did it because he wanted to make Israel his holy sanctuary. He wanted a people of his very own, marked by his undeserving love, favored with his glorious presence. Truly God is not a distant monarch, far above the heavens, but a Servant King, present on the earth. "He is near" (v. 8).

Ask God to show you his nearness to you and your dearness to him.

What do you see?

_____

_____

_____

_____

_____

_____

_____

_____

_____

_____

_____

_____

_____

_____

_____

_____

_____

Passionate Love

PSALMS 115–116

Psalm 115 begins: "You are the One who loves us passionately" (v. 1). Once a person has encountered this divine love, they have a testimony no unbeliever can destroy. Unbelievers worship the created, not the Creator, and as such, the object of their idolatry cannot speak to them or hear them. We, on the other hand, worship the Creator, and he is personal and loving; he hears and answers us. This God wraps his presence around his lovers and gives them not only a great intimacy but a great authority: the heavens belong to him, but the earth belongs to us (v. 16). Let's welcome the fire of God's passionate love into our hearts every day.

While Psalm 115 begins with the revelation of God's passionate love for us, Psalm 116 begins with an expression of our passionate love for him: "I am passionately in love with God" (v. 1). God's lovers are people who know him personally and experientially. They are people who vow, "As long as I live, I'll keep praying to him." They are the childlike and humble ones who know what it is to be low before him, broken and desperate. They also know what it is to be lifted from their striving to a place of quiet rest in him. Such lovers have an unsophisticated trust in the Father and position themselves day and night before his life-giving light. Whenever a lover like this dies, it touches God's heart (v. 15). Let's live life to the end, loving God.

"I am passionately in love with God." Turn this phrase into your own cry of worship and allow the Holy Spirit to blow upon the embers of your heart until you are aflame with love again.

The Gateway to God

PSALMS 117–118

There is one key guaranteed to unlock the great doors into God's majestic presence: high praise. Psalm 117 is high praise. The songwriter begins by inviting everyone to be luminous with praise. The idea of shining is contained within the Hebrew word for "praise." The object of the psalmist's praise is God's love and his kindness. He has conquered us with his love and melted our hearts with his kindness. Kindness is a glorious word. It refers to the mercy that God in his covenant has pledged himself to show to his people. Aren't you grateful that God is kind? What a beautiful word *kindness* is. What a priceless virtue. What a rare commodity in our brutal world. Let's open the vast gates into God's royal halls with passionate and high praise of God's kindness. As Psalm 117 reveals, our praise doesn't have to be wordy, just shiny!

When we begin to praise God for the glorious things he's done in our lives, the gates into his presence swing very wide. Psalm 118 is full of such praise. The songwriter one time had an experience of being hemmed in, trapped, surrounded, and diminished. But he prayed to God, and God came to help him like a loving father. He released him from his place of restriction and set him in a beautiful and broad place. His repeated cry of praise is therefore that God's tender and constant love lasts forever! God is his Valiant Warrior whose supernatural power set him free. "I have found the gateway to God, the pathway to his presence for all his lovers," he exclaims (v. 20). That gateway is the place of "loving praise." Loving praise brings people into the presence of the Sent One of the Lord (Jesus). Let's cultivate this kind of high praise in our lives.

"I will offer my loving praise to you." Notice that this is a choice the writer makes. Make this your choice and enjoy more of his lovely presence as you release more of your loving praise.

_____

_____

_____

_____

_____

_____

_____

_____

_____

_____

_____

_____

_____

_____

Passion for His Precepts

PSALMS 119-120

One of the hallmarks of a genuine move of the Holy Spirit is a love for God's Word among his people. In Psalm 119, King David articulates his love for the Scriptures. God's Word is perfect and infallible. It is the greatest treasure, a shining light for those with open hearts. Those who walk in alignment with God's Word experience strength, honor, abundance, and joy. They experience revival as they read and apply the Scriptures. David was passionate for God's precepts; he yearned for revelation light. He knew that God's Word is fastened to eternity (v. 89), so he filled his heart with its truth. "I'm a lover of your Word," he proclaimed. Those who can say that with passion will live constantly in an atmosphere of revival.

One of the many reasons David gives in Psalm 119 for loving the Scriptures is that God's Word keeps us in alignment with God's ways when we are being unjustly treated. In Psalm 119:114, David speaks of how he wraps himself in God's Word when he is attacked by the wicked. In this way, his mind is set on responding in the Spirit rather than reacting in the flesh. Psalm 120 is a vivid example of this. The songwriter is desperate, struggling in the face of false accusation. What is he to do? Lying deceivers—people who hate peace—are out to get him. In the heart of darkness, the psalmist makes a choice. While his enemies speak words of war, he speaks words of peace. Those who have a passion for God's Word will always discover the countercultural wisdom of heaven. Let's allow our passion for God's Word to grow so that our perspective on life's struggles can shift to match our Father's.

"My passion and delight is in your Word, for I love what you say to me! I long for more revelation of your truth, for I love the light of your Word as I meditate on your decrees" (Psalm 119:47–48). Turn these verses into your own prayer today.

_____

_____

_____

_____

_____

_____

_____

_____

_____

_____

_____

_____

_____

_____

_____

_____

The True Place of Peace

PSALMS 121–122

Psalms 120 to 134 are known as songs of "ascent" or "songs to take you higher." If ever there was a song designed to lift us up, Psalm 121 is it. The original context was probably the pilgrim's journey up to Jerusalem for the Feasts of the Lord: Passover, Pentecost, and Tabernacles. The pilgrim may even have recited these songs climbing up the steps toward the temple. As the pilgrim looked up, he realized once again that his protection did not come from the mountains and hills but from God, who tirelessly watches over us all day and night. Let's never forget that God is by our side at all times. He watches over us and shelters us. Guarded by God himself, we find a place of peace under the canopy of his vigilant love.

It's not easy to find a place of untroubled serenity in a turbulent world like ours. In the day of the psalmist, Jerusalem was associated with God's peace (Psalm 122). If you look at the end of the name, it sounds like the Hebrew word *shalom*, translated "peace." Jerusalem was built as a city where God and man could mingle together, a place of pilgrimage where Jehovah God could be forever worshiped. It was created to be the City of Peace. How sad it is to see that Jerusalem today is a city where security and tranquility are achieved through weapons rather than trusting in God's holy presence. We should pray for the peace of Jerusalem, and at the same time remember that our peace is in the arms of our Guardian God.

Our peace is found in the arms of Jesus, who is the Prince of Peace. Bring all your troubles and cares to him and ask him for the heavenly peace that passes all understanding—a peace that the world cannot give.

Always There

PSALMS 123–124

*A*s the sons and daughters of God, we can boldly approach the throne of God any time. That is a heartening truth. In Psalm 123 the psalmist approaches God with the inspiring address, "O God-Enthroned in heaven" (v. 1). He comes before God with two great longings: first to please him; second, to dig more deeply into the revelation of God's mercy and grace. Those are two great passions: the first is to make our Father happy; the second is to find out more about his affectionate, lavish heart of love toward us. As we live to please him—as a servant lives to please his master—we encounter more and more of his undeserved love, especially when others mistreat us. We learn, in short, that he is always there.

*A*re you ready to go higher? Psalm 124 is another song of ascent, another "song of the stairway" (that is to say, a song originally sung while climbing the steps to the temple). Here David gives praise to God because he was always there. If God had not been there for Israel, then their enemies would have devoured them. But God was there to defend and protect them. He is the one who has promised never to leave nor forsake his people. The same God who put the planets in orbit and created the deepest depths of the oceans is also our Helper and Defender. That makes all the difference. It is always a salutary thing to ask the psalmist's question: "What if God had not been on our side?" (v. 1).

Look back on your life and ask the question, "What if God had not been there for me?" Turn your gratitude into passionate prayer, giving thanks to God for being your Helper and Defender.

_____

_____

_____

_____

_____

_____

_____

_____

_____

_____

_____

_____

_____

_____

_____

Surprised by Joy
PSALMS 125–126

One of the greatest experiences a human being can have is the feeling of being encircled and enfolded by the presence of God. In Psalm 125 we climb yet higher into heaven's glorious truths as the songwriter gives praise to God for his "wrap-around presence." This is a beautiful phrase, one that pulls us into the joy of our Father's loving arms. King David knew what this felt like. He had encountered it many times. He summed it up with a perfect simile: just as the mountains surround Jerusalem, so the arms of the Father surround his godly lovers. Safe within those arms, we enjoy two things: peace and prosperity. We enjoy a sense of harmony with God and with others (and indeed with ourselves) and a sense of God's favor. There is such joy in the all-encompassing embrace of Father God.

Joy is one of the great hallmarks of a revived soul and a revived community. Psalm 126 gives eloquent voice to this revival joy. To be sure, this kind of euphoric joy in the Lord is often preceded by intense weeping over sin and its consequences. But these tears are not the end game. God is a lavishly loving restorer of souls. When we break through from weeping to laughing, it is like a dream come true. We laugh, we shout, we sing! We begin to pray for a fresh revelation of God's glory. We cry out for God's streams of refreshing to soak us. Those who sow tears like seed in the ground will always be blessed beyond all description. They will "reap a harvest with joyful shouts of glee" (v. 5). Let's get sowing so that we may know the ebullient and ecstatic joy of the harvest.

If you've sown tears, you will reap joy. Spend some time praying for the Holy Spirit to give you a fresh and joyful revelation of the encircling arms of God's affectionate love.

Family Blessings

PSALMS 127–128

There are so many blessings God has in store for his lovers. In Psalm 127 the songwriter describes a number of what we might call "family blessings." In verse 2 he tells us that God will always provide for his lovers, so there is no need to be afraid of not having enough. Such a fear will drive us to toil to make a living and show that we are driven by fear rather than led by love. Furthermore, God's lovers will have the great blessing of children. They are "heaven's generous reward" and "a love-gift from God" (v. 3). The promise given to all who love God and have children is this: "Your kids will have influence and honor" (v. 5). If you don't have children of your own yet, claim this promise for others.

Psalm 128 describes yet more "family blessings." For those who love the Lord and bow low before him, there are material blessings (prosperity), emotional blessings (happiness), and spiritual blessings (well-being). Then there are marital blessings (your wife will bless your heart and home) and parental blessings (your children will bring you great joy around the family meal table). The songwriter ends by praying a wonderful benediction on those who love God: "May you be surrounded by your grandchildren" (v. 6). Aren't you grateful that you have a heavenly Father who longs to bless you? Aren't you glad that these rewards begin at home, with "family blessings"? It's time to count our blessings again.

See your family through God's eyes. Envision your family exemplifying
the beauty of God's family portrait in Psalms 127–128.
What does that look like?

The Miracle That Is Israel

PSALMS 129–130

There are many views held by Christians about Israel, but one thing we can all marvel at is the extraordinary durability of this tiny nation. While far greater empires have come and gone, Israel has somehow miraculously survived. This is a thought that grips the songwriter in Psalm 129. From the beginning Israel has experienced persecution and discrimination, and yet she has survived. "We're still here!" the psalmist cries (v. 2). God has always stood to defend his people against those who hate the Jews. What's the secret? Psalm 129 answers the question. God's supernatural, covenant love is the secret.

It is a perplexing thing to realize on the one hand that God has so evidently preserved the people of Israel and on the other that the Jewish people in the state of Israel today are among the most secular on the earth. How can this be? Psalm 130 provides an answer. It is purely and simply down to the forgiving love of God. If God had marked and measured Israel by the number of her sins, no prayers prayed by Jewish people would ever be answered. But God is forgiving, loving, gracious, and merciful. His love is a love that will not let his people go, in spite of their sins. All he is waiting for is for his people to long for him as a watchman longs for the morning light. His word is this: "O Israel . . . keep waiting on the Lord" (v. 7). Let's pray this over the Jewish people that they may see that Jesus is Messiah and Lord.

God is breathing his Holy Spirit into many Jewish people today, inside and outside of Israel. Pray with passion for Jewish people you know to come to know who Jesus really was and is.

The Resting Place
PSALMS 131–132

Where truly is our heart's home? According to the Bible, it is in the arms of God. As the early church theologian St. Augustine once said, "Our hearts are restless until they find their rest in you." The heart only comes to a place of serenity when its rebellion has come to an end. This is exactly what King David is saying in Psalm 131. David has stopped trying to understand mysteries that are too complex. His heart has now found peace and quiet in the arms of God. He is now contented and at rest, like an infant at the breast of his nursing, soothing, and affectionate mother. This is true for all of us. The heart's home is in the loving arms of God. When we become "a resting child," our souls discover true contentment. Let's live from that place of rest.

If Psalm 131 is about our resting place with God, Psalm 132 is about God's resting place with us. This song goes back to King David's longing to build a resting place for the presence of God. He would not rest in his own house until he had built a house on earth in which God could dwell. "I devote myself to finding a resting place for you," he cried (v. 5). That longing was fulfilled when the temple was built in Jerusalem by King Solomon. There God's "glistening glory" rested upon his chosen ones. All this leads to a profound truth: if it is important for us to find a resting place *in* God, it is equally important for us to create a resting place *for* God. Let's create such places and cry out with the psalmist: "Arise, O Lord, and enter your resting place!" (v. 8).

Spend a few moments thanking God that not only does he love us like no earthly father ever could, but he also loves us like no earthly mother could.

Dripping with God's Blessing

PSALMS 133-134

Have you ever wondered if there's a way you can secure the release of God's blessing over your life? If so, Psalm 133 provides at least one answer. When brothers and sisters in Christ live together in sweet unity, then God releases his blessing. This blessing is like the anointing oil that dripped from the top of Aaron's head to the hem of his robes. It's like the dew that drips from the heavens and brings refreshment to the slopes of Mount Hermon. If we want to receive the blessing of God, we could start by committing ourselves to sweet unity with other believers. Disunity and division drive God's blessings away. But when unity is restored, the anointing is released and drips from heaven onto our heads until we are covered in its fragrance.

Another way to receive God's blessing is through sacrificial praise. There's something about going the extra mile in praise that attracts blessing and breakthrough. Remember Paul and Silas in prison in Philippi? They were singing God's praise at midnight while they were in the stocks in prison. God responded with awesome power (Acts 16:26). In Psalm 134 the songwriter encourages God's loving priests to praise God in the watches of the night. Lifting up holy hands in worship during the night, we bless God deeply and in the process attract his blessings. Let's do this more often. If we can't sleep, let's turn frustration into adoration. If the Holy Spirit wakes us up, let's turn interruption into intercession. In the process, we will fulfill our calling as loving priests and priestly lovers, and we will drip with God's blessing.

The next time you are up at night, bring your expressions of affection to God as a loving priest. What might you say?

_____

_____

_____

_____

_____

_____

_____

_____

_____

_____

_____

_____

_____

_____

_____

A Lofty and Lowly Love
PSALMS 135-136

If ever you needed a great reason for thanking God, you'll find one in Psalm 135. Here the songwriter tells us time and again how great, mighty, and awesome God is. He is the King because he can do what he pleases. He is the Creator because he makes the thunder and lightning. He is the Judge because he punishes those who oppose him. He is the Miracle Worker because he performs signs and wonders. He is the Conqueror because he defeats his enemies. He is alive because (unlike idols) he hears our prayers and speaks to our hearts. He is Lord Yahweh because he reigns over all the earth. Yet, at the same time, God loves us individually. He has time for us. He regards us as "his special treasure" (v. 4). The God of the Universe holds you in the palm of his hand like a priceless gemstone and says, "You're so special to me." How unspeakably wonderful that this God is our Father!

Everyone loves to be thanked, and God is no exception. Psalm 136 begins, "Let everyone thank God, for he is good." The songwriter then lists reasons why we should be grateful: God is king over all gods, he is Lord of Lords, the miracle-working Lord, the Creator who has filled the heavens with revelation, the Deliverer of his children, the Leader of his people, the Vanquisher of his enemies, and the Great Provider. Above all, he is the one "who chose us when we were nothing!" (v. 23). You were *nothing*, but God came looking for you, rescued you, adopted you, and made *something* out of you. Let's live in constant gratitude.

Listen to God's word of affirmation over you: "You're my special treasure." How does it make you feel to be so treasured by the infinite and all-powerful God? Turn your response into heartfelt thanksgiving.

_____

_____

_____

_____

_____

_____

_____

_____

_____

_____

_____

_____

_____

_____

_____

Real, Not Robotic Lovers

PSALMS 137–138

*G*od never wanted robotic lovers. His heart was always for us to respond out of our own will with a choice to love him and a decision to give him praise, especially when the days are dark and times are tough. And they are tough in Psalm 137. God's people are in exile in Babylon (modern Iraq), homesick for Jerusalem, mourning for Zion. Those who have taken them captive are mocking them: "Sing one of your happy Zion songs!" they shout. Everything within the psalmist tells him that it's time to hang up his harp in the willow trees and stop singing. But the songwriter activates his free will and makes a choice to not forget Jerusalem, to not neglect to sing his song. He will keep loving, praising, and trusting God. Let's say, "I will give him praise" every day, however tough it is.

*T*here is no situation so bleak, so terrifying, so depressing, and so awful that we cannot choose to give God praise and see him respond with power. As the songwriter puts it in Psalm 138, "Through your mighty power I can walk through any devastation, and you will keep me alive, reviving me" (v. 7). In even the most distressing circumstances, we can choose to thank the Lord with all the passion of our hearts. At the very moment when we call out like this, God hears us and strengthens us deep within our souls. He proves that he is true to his promises, and he refreshes us with his constant and tender love. However difficult life is, let's use the gift of free will wisely. Let's say, "I will praise him" and watch as God finishes every good work that he's begun in us.

When you find worship a challenge, say, "I choose to bless the Lord! I will give God praise!" As you do, watch as God's reviving power begins to flow into even the weariest part of your being.

_____

_____

_____

_____

_____

_____

_____

_____

_____

_____

_____

_____

_____

_____

Lovers of God's Presence

PSALMS 139–140

God's presence is everywhere. There's nowhere we can go where his Spirit cannot be encountered—not in the shining dawn or the radiant sunset. As David says in Psalm 139, "Your presence is everywhere" (v. 11). At the same time, David knows another dimension to God's presence—a more intimate and intense dimension in which God's love is shown to him personally. When David moves into this kind of encounter, he experiences a revelation of the Father's unique love for him. He knows that he is the object of God's doting and detailed gaze. He knows that nothing has been hidden from the Father's eyes since the beginning. So he prays: "Examine me through and through" (v. 23). Let's hunger more for this intimate and intense dimension of God's presence.

The only antidote to intimidation from people is the intimacy of God's presence. Even when our enemies are all around us, we can have a party in God's presence. This is very much the theme of Psalm 140. Once again David is under attack. But in the midst of conflict, David positions his soul in a place of peace and security. In the heat of the battle, he encounters the wraparound presence of God. This is what godly lovers always do "because they choose and cherish your presence above everything else!" (v. 13). Let's cherish God's intense and intimate presence, valuing that above all other things in our lives. Our gratitude opens up the portals into his love, and there we feast even in the presence of our foes.

"You cherish me constantly in every thought!" You are God's happy and constant thought. How does that make you feel? Turn your emotion into devotion as you ponder these things in your heart.

_____

_____

_____

_____

_____

_____

_____

_____

_____

_____

_____

_____

_____

_____

_____

The Only One

PSALMS 141–142

In biblical times, a woman who had become betrothed to a man went around in public wearing a veil. That veil was a code; in Hebrew it said *mekudheshet*, or "I'm spoken for." It was her way of saying that her eyes were now reserved exclusively for her bridegroom. In Psalm 141, King David makes this passionate statement: "You are my Lord and my God; I only have eyes for you" (v. 8). David utters this cry in a time of difficulty and danger. He is surrounded by "experts in evil" who want to entice and entrap him. But David resolves to keep his eyes fixed on the Lord. He will not fall into their traps. He knows how a person's eyes can lead them into sin. So he fixes his attention and affection in an exclusive way on God. In the same way, guard your eyes and say, "I only have eyes for you."

When you fall in love and get married, your love for your spouse becomes exclusive. The same should be true when we fall in love with God. God is jealous for our affections. When it comes to worship, he wants us to have eyes for him alone. So when King David is hiding in a cave and begins to pray (Psalm 142), it would have brought God deep delight when David confesses that God is "the only One" (v. 3). For David, he was the only One to help and protect him. He was "the only One" present when David was in confinement and isolation. He was "the only One" to whom David could call out for help. Our intimacy with God goes to a whole new level when we start to praise him as "the only One" we worship. God loves it when he hears our hearts cry, "You're all I have."

God wants an exclusive love. He wants us to have eyes only for him. Ask him if there are any areas in your life that draw your affection away from him alone. Confess those areas and ask him to remove those idols from your heart. Then say to him, "You're the only One."

In Times of Trouble

PSALMS 143–144

*C*oming to a genuine faith in God does not inoculate you from life's troubles; it gives you faith for enduring and overcoming them. In Psalm 143, David is being pursued by Absalom and he is in big trouble. He is in danger. He is facing death. He is experiencing depression. He is caving in to despair. What is he to do? He does the only thing he knows. He reaches out to God, thirsting for his presence. "Your gracious Spirit is all I need" (v. 10). He expresses his desperation for God, saying that he longs for God "like the dry, cracked ground thirsts for rain" (v. 6). The one thing he can hold onto is God's promises. He appeals to these, knowing that God cannot break his word. This gives him the impetus to look forward in faith, anticipating a new dawn in which God's tender love will be revealed. Let's activate our faith in God's promises in times of trouble.

*H*ow would you feel if you were a young lad with a sling facing a huge giant with a sword? Psalm 144 is said to be King David's prayer before he engaged in mortal combat with Goliath, the gargantuan champion of the Philistines. As David stands in the shadow of the giant, he looks up. He doesn't look at the giant but at One greater. There's only one safe place, he says, and that's God, "and I love him" (v. 1). David hides himself in God and then prays for a revelation of God's victorious strength and for deliverance from the dark powers set against him. He determines that he will sing a new song when God grants him the victory. What gigantic faith David shows here. Instead of saying, "Look how big Goliath is!" he says, "Look how big my God is!" When we face big troubles, let's always exercise big faith.

Is there some gigantic trouble that you're facing right now? If so, write down any promises that God has spoken over your life and turn these into prayers of faith. Don't tell God how big the problems are. Tell the problems how big God is!

_____

_____

_____

_____

_____

_____

_____

_____

_____

_____

_____

_____

_____

_____

Praise and High Praise

PSALMS 145-146

There's praise and then there's high praise. Praise is a discipline. High praise is a delight. In Psalm 145, David moves from the duty of praise into the ecstasy of high praise. He says that his heart explodes with praise. He cannot take in how utterly and indescribably great God is. He is overwhelmed with God's goodness, his glory, and his awe-inspiring acts of power. David's heart bubbles over as he meditates on God's "excellent greatness" and his "marvelous beauty" (vv. 6-7). God's love is like a river of kindness that constantly overflows its banks. In fact, God manifests himself as kindness in everything he does. See how the heart explodes in this psalm? When we are wrecked by the revelation of God's greatness, we move from sacrificial duty to euphoric delight. We move from praise to high praise.

If we need some reasons for entering into high praise, David gives us a whole raft of them in Psalm 146. God is worthy of our high praise (the praise of our "innermost being") because unlike earthly leaders who are mortal and fallible, he never fails us. He keeps his promises. He is the Creator of heaven's glory and earth's grandeur. He brings justice to those whom society neglects and despises. He heals the sick. He feeds the hungry. He restores the fallen. He watches over immigrants and supports the orphan and the widow. He subverts the plans of the ungodly, and he reigns forever and ever. David says that he will spend every day of his life giving God praise. It's hard to think of a grander purpose or a greater resolution than this. Let's give God the highest praise every day.

Draw near afresh to God. He will reveal himself to you afresh. Then let your heart bubble over in high praise and move from duty to delight.

A Beautifying Power

PSALMS 147–148

Have you ever tried to make yourself look more beautiful? There is one thing that always succeeds in renewing your youth and making you radiant—the beautifying power of praise. As David says in Psalm 147, it is a beautiful thing to bring our praises to a beautiful God. When we do, praise makes us lovely before him. It beautifies us in a way that nothing else can. This is because we were created to marvel at the beauty of our Creator. God has been consumed with bringing beauty to his creation since the beginning of time. When we give ourselves to praise, he beautifies us as well. The Divine Artist, who paints the landscape with frost, fills our hearts with color and our faces with his heavenly radiance. Let's beautify ourselves with praise!

When we yield ourselves to the beautifying power of praise, we cannot help but marvel at God's creation. The whole universe is elegant. Everything God has made is a masterpiece, resonant with truth and vibrant with beauty. Therefore, as Psalm 148 reveals, our worship can never be a purely isolated act. We are compelled by the beauty of God to invite the whole of creation into joining us in praise. We command the sun and moon to worship, the great pelagic fish to echo in exultation. We exhort birds and beasts, mice and men, to give God praise. As we lead this orchestra of cosmic praise, God's favor and strength begin to anoint us. As we conduct God's beautiful creation in worship, we are beautified and renewed by praise.

There is nothing healthier than giving God the highest praise. Reflect on the truth that praise beautifies you, and then let thankfulness rise up within you as you worship God.

Enthused with Joy

PSALMS 149–150

How wonderful it is to end our devotional readings of the Psalms on a note of intense joy. Psalm 149 begins with an inspiring invitation to give our hallelujah to God. "May Israel be enthused with joy," the songwriter proclaims (v. 2). What a phrase that is—"enthused with joy." To be enthused with joy is to be filled with such a sense of the goodness of God that you cannot stop yourself from praising him. When God pours his Spirit into us, we are filled so full with the revelation of God's kindness that joyful songs of praise begin to overflow from our mouths. As the Spirit moves us to meditate on the way God adorns the humble with his beauty, we become so much more than religion could ever make us. We become godly lovers who triumph in the glory of God, singing songs that bring deliverance.

The book of Psalms ends with an invitation to ecstatic praise (Psalm 150). The *contexts* for praise are ubiquitous. Praise can be given to God anytime and anywhere, whether on earth in God's house or in heaven in his stronghold. The *reasons* for praise are manifold. You can praise God for anything or everything, from his miracles of might to his magnificent greatness. The *instruments* for praise are endless—ranging from pianos and guitars to drums and trumpets. The *methods* of praise are varied too, whether you are dancing before the Lord or making music and song. Everyone, everywhere, can bring God ecstatic praise. Let them be a crescendo—an ever-increasing, ever-expanding shout of praise. Let them above all be characterized by this one great thing: that they are "enthused with joy."

Ask the Holy Spirit to enthuse you with joy. Release your ecstatic praise to God. Let your awe and thankfulness and celebration of his goodness burst forth from you in every way you can imagine!

_____

_____

_____

_____

_____

_____

_____

_____

_____

_____

_____

_____

_____

_____

_____

_____

_____

_____

My Thoughts

My Thoughts

My Thoughts